Inside AI

Understanding the Technology that Drives Intelligence

Edwin Crowe

Table of Contents

Roadmap

Inside AI

Understanding the Technology that Drives Intelligence

Purpose of This Book

To explore, explain, and demystify artificial intelligence, from its mythic beginnings to the cutting-edge technologies reshaping our world. This book strikes a balance between technical depth and clarity, aiming to both educate and inspire. It is a journey through the science, philosophy, and societal impact of intelligent machines, accessible to the curious, engaging to the tech-savvy, and grounded in storytelling and real-world relevance.

Structural Overview

Part I: The Roots of Intelligence

Tracing the historical, philosophical, and conceptual foundations of AI.

- **The Dream of Thinking Machines**
  — From ancient myths and mechanical marvels to Alan Turing and the birth of computational intelligence.
- **Learning to Learn**
  — How machines learn from data: an introduction to supervised, unsupervised, and reinforcement learning.
- **Inside the Neural Network**
  — Exploring artificial neurons, network architectures, and the foundations of deep learning.
- **Transformers**
  — The revolution in modern AI: attention mechanisms, language understanding, and models like GPT and BERT.

Part II: Inside AI Systems

How Machines Learn and Work

The practical blueprint of applied AI—deployment, ethics, and explainability.

- **Deploying AI in the Real World**
  From research prototypes to operational systems: infrastructure, data pipelines, and edge intelligence.
- **Explainable AI**
  Making the black box visible: interpretability, transparency, and building trust in AI decisions.
- **Ethical Intelligence**
  Ensuring fairness, accountability, privacy, and human oversight in an increasingly automated world.

Part III: AI Tomorrow

Imagination, Innovation, and the Unknown

A forward-looking exploration of AI's frontiers and its impact on creativity, society, and human potential.

- **The Next Wave**
  Breakthroughs in self-supervised learning, foundation models, neurosymbolic AI, and AI for scientific discovery.
- **Multimodal and Embodied AI**
  Integrating vision, language, sound, and motion—machines that perceive and act in the real world.
- **AI and Creativity**
  Generative AI and the redefinition of art, music, storytelling, and human expression.
- **Artificial General Intelligence**
  The pursuit of machines that reason, adapt, and think across domains—myth, reality, or inevitability?
- **Coexistence**
  The human-AI partnership: designing futures of collaboration, augmentation, and shared progress.

Appendices A to I

Deeper Dive Reference Guide

Appendices A–F
Core foundations of AI:
Key concepts, neural architectures, learning algorithms, data workflows, evaluation metrics, and explainability tools.

Appendices G–I
Essential research resources:
Benchmark datasets, historical milestones, and glossary-style summaries for deeper technical exploration.

A Journey from Origins to
Explainable Intelligence

Part I

The Roots of Intelligence

A Brief History of AI

Chapter 1

The Dream of Thinking Machines

The Timeless Fascination with Intelligent Beings

For as long as humanity has told stories, we've dreamed of creating life in our own image—intelligent beings capable of thought, reason, and emotion. Across civilizations and centuries, these dreams surfaced in myths and legends. Ancient Jewish folklore spoke of the Golem, a figure of clay brought to life to protect the people. Greek mythology described Hephaestus forging mechanical servants of gold to assist him. In China, legends told of Yan Shi, an artificer who created a life-sized automaton, capable of movement and speech. Indian mythology spoke of the *bhuta-vahana-yanta*, machines said to guard treasures in temples.

These tales reflected a universal fascination with the possibility of crafting intelligence, blending the magical with the mechanical. But they remained firmly in the realm of myth.

Centuries later, during the Age of Enlightenment, inventors began designing intricate mechanical automata. Jacques de Vaucanson's Digesting Duck—a mechanical marvel that mimicked eating and digestion—and Pierre Jaquet-Droz's

9

writing automaton captivated the public. Though lifelike in their actions, they did not think. The dream of an intelligent machine, a true thinking entity, remained elusive.

The Birth of a New Science

By the early 20th century, the foundation for true machine intelligence was finally taking shape. Advances in mathematics, logic, and early computers hinted that the age-old dream might be within reach.

One man, Alan Turing, would profoundly shape this vision. During World War II, Turing's work in breaking the Enigma code saved countless lives and showcased the potential of machines to solve complex problems. In 1950, he posed a provocative question in his paper "Computing Machinery and Intelligence": "Can machines think?"

Rather than debating consciousness, Turing reframed the question in behavioral terms. He proposed what would later be called the Turing Test: if a machine could respond in a conversation indistinguishably from a human, should we not consider it intelligent? This simple yet powerful idea became a cornerstone in the field that was about to be born.

The Dartmouth Conference: The Birth of Artificial Intelligence

In 1956, four pioneers—John McCarthy, Marvin Minsky, Nathaniel Rochester, and Claude Shannon—organized a workshop at Dartmouth College. They proposed an ambitious idea: "Every aspect of learning or any other feature of intelligence can in principle be so precisely described that a machine can be made to simulate it."

This summer workshop marked the official birth of Artificial Intelligence as a field of study.

The term "artificial intelligence" was coined, and with it came a wave of optimism. The researchers believed that human-level machine intelligence was achievable within a generation.

Their bold vision ignited public imagination and secured early funding. AI quickly became the focus of major research initiatives, as governments and universities competed to unlock its potential.

Early Breakthroughs and the First AI Winter

The early years of AI research were filled with excitement and breakthroughs. Programs like Logic Theorist and General Problem Solver demonstrated that machines could reason through complex problems. ELIZA, created by Joseph Weizenbaum in the 1960s, could simulate a psychotherapy session using simple keyword recognition. To many, ELIZA felt uncannily human.

Yet, despite these advances, AI systems faced significant limitations. They struggled with tasks requiring common sense, contextual understanding, or flexible adaptation to new situations. While a program could excel at a narrow task like chess, it lacked the broader reasoning abilities of a human being.

As progress slowed, funding diminished. The early promises had outpaced reality. The 1970s ushered in what became known as the first "AI Winter"—a period marked by disappointment and reduced investment.

Revivals and Renaissance

AI saw a revival in the 1980s with the rise of expert systems. These programs, like MYCIN, could emulate the decision-making process of human experts using carefully curated rules. In medicine and industry, expert systems showed promise, diagnosing diseases and guiding complex operations.

But expert systems had their limitations. They were brittle, struggled with uncertainty, and required extensive manual updates. Once again, AI hit a ceiling.

In the late 1990s and early 2000s, three forces converged to spark a new AI renaissance: exponential increases in computing power, the explosion of digital data, and advances in machine learning algorithms. The era of "big data" and neural networks had arrived.

One milestone moment was IBM's Deep Blue defeating world chess champion Garry Kasparov in 1997. For the first time, a machine had outmatched a human grandmaster. It was a narrow domain, but the implications were profound.

The Rise of the Black Box

As AI systems became more powerful, they also became more complex—and less transparent. Deep learning algorithms, while achieving remarkable accuracy, operated as "black boxes." Even the engineers who built them often couldn't explain how they made specific decisions.

This opacity sparked concern. In fields like healthcare and finance, where AI was increasingly making high-stakes decisions, the inability to explain *why* a machine made a particular recommendation became a serious ethical and practical issue.

One notable example is healthcare AI used to predict patient outcomes. In some cases, systems made life-and-death recommendations without providing doctors with interpretable reasoning. Without transparency, trust eroded.

Toward Explainable Intelligence

Today, the AI community is focused not just on building smarter systems, but on making them understandable. Explainable AI (XAI) aims to open up the black box, providing insights into how AI systems arrive at their decisions. Transparency, accountability, and fairness have become guiding principles.

The journey from the ancient legends of thinking machines to modern AI is an extraordinary story of human curiosity and ingenuity. But the next chapter may be the most important: building AI we can trust.

In the chapters that follow, we'll go deeper into how AI works, why explainability matters, and how the technology that drives intelligence is shaping the world around us.

Chapter 2

Learning to Learn

Algorithms That Improve Over Time

What Does It Mean to Learn?

Imagine teaching a child to recognize an apple. You don't hand them a dictionary definition or a complex set of instructions. Instead, you show them examples: red apples, green apples, big ones, small ones. Over time, they learn to recognize apples on their own, even ones they've never seen before. This simple concept—learning from examples—is at the heart of machine learning (ML).

Unlike traditional computer programs, which follow explicitly written rules, machine learning enables computers to learn patterns and make decisions from data. Instead of programming a system *how* to solve a problem, we program it *how to learn* from experience. This shift is fundamental to the rise of artificial intelligence.

The Three Main Types of Machine Learning

AI systems typically learn in three primary ways: supervised learning, unsupervised learning, and reinforcement learning. Each approach teaches machines differently, depending on the type of problem and data available.

1) Supervised Learning: Learning with Guidance

Supervised learning is like learning with a teacher. Imagine sorting pictures of animals with someone guiding you: "This is a cat," "That is a dog." Over time, you get better at distinguishing between them. Supervised learning works the same way. Machines are fed data that comes with labels—examples where the correct answers are already known.

The goal is to find the underlying patterns that link inputs to outputs. Spam filters, speech recognition, and disease diagnosis systems often use supervised learning. For example, a spam filter might learn from thousands of labeled emails ("spam" or "not spam") and then predict whether a new email is spam.

---

2) Unsupervised Learning: Finding Patterns on Its Own

Unsupervised learning happens without guidance—no labels, no right answers provided. Instead, the system explores the data, finding hidden patterns or groupings by itself.

A good example is customer segmentation. Given purchasing data, an unsupervised learning algorithm can group customers with similar behaviors—without knowing in advance who belongs in which group. These insights help businesses target their marketing more effectively.

Unsupervised learning is also used in anomaly detection (spotting fraudulent credit card transactions) and data compression (reducing file sizes without losing essential information).

3Reinforcement Learning: Learning from Experience

Reinforcement learning (RL) mimics how humans and animals learn from consequences. Picture a dog learning tricks: when it sits on command, it gets a treat; when it disobeys, there's no reward. Over time, it learns which behaviors lead to good outcomes.

In reinforcement learning, an AI agent interacts with an environment, making decisions and receiving rewards (positive feedback) or penalties (negative feedback). Its goal is to maximize rewards over time by learning the best strategies.

Reinforcement learning powers autonomous vehicles, robotic control systems, and game-playing AIs like DeepMind's AlphaGo, which we'll explore shortly.

Key Algorithms—Explained Simply

At the heart of machine learning are algorithms—systems that learn from data and make predictions. Let's take a closer look at a few fundamental ones.

1) Decision Trees: The Flowchart of Decisions

Think of a decision tree as a series of yes/no questions that guide you to an answer. It's like playing 20 Questions. For example, to classify an animal, the tree might ask: "Does it have fur?" If yes, "Does it bark?" Each answer leads you down a branch until you reach a decision.

Decision trees are easy to understand and interpret. They're widely used in medical diagnosis and financial risk assessments because their reasoning is transparent and explainable.

---

2) k-Nearest Neighbors (k-NN): Learning from Neighbors

Imagine moving to a new city and asking nearby locals where to find a good coffee shop. You trust their answers because they're close to you and know the area well. k-Nearest Neighbors works on the same principle.

Given a new data point, it finds the "k" closest points in its dataset and makes a prediction based on their outcomes. k-NN is simple and effective for tasks like handwriting recognition or classifying images but can be slow with very large datasets.

---

3) Support Vector Machines (SVM): Drawing the Perfect Boundary

Support Vector Machines find the best possible boundary—or line—that separates data into categories. Imagine sorting apples and oranges by drawing a line on a graph.

SVM chooses the line that maximizes the distance between the closest points on either side.

SVM works well in high-dimensional spaces and is often used for tasks like text classification, where data can have thousands of features (words or terms).

A Story of Success: AlphaGo and the Reinforcement Learning Revolution

One of the most celebrated success stories of reinforcement learning is AlphaGo. Developed by DeepMind, AlphaGo defeated Lee Sedol, one of the world's greatest Go players, in 2016. Go is an ancient and complex board game, far more challenging for computers than chess because of its vast number of possible moves.

AlphaGo learned to play by combining reinforcement learning with deep neural networks. It played millions of games against itself, learning strategies and refining its skills with each match. What stunned experts was AlphaGo's ability to develop unconventional moves and strategies that even human masters had never seen.

This victory was a turning point in AI. It showed that machines could not only master complex tasks but also innovate—finding solutions that humans might never have considered.

Why Explainability Matters

As machine learning models grow in complexity, understanding *why* they make decisions becomes more difficult. Many powerful algorithms—especially deep learning systems—are often criticized as "black boxes" because their inner workings are opaque.

This lack of transparency is a problem in high-stakes fields like healthcare, finance, and law. For example, if an AI recommends a treatment for a patient, doctors need to understand the reasoning behind the suggestion. Was it based on the patient's history, lab results, or something else?

Explainable AI (XAI) focuses on making these decisions understandable. Simple models like decision trees are inherently transparent, but more complex models require additional tools. Techniques like SHAP (SHapley Additive exPlanations) and LIME (Local Interpretable Model-agnostic Explanations) help shed light on which factors influenced a decision.

By providing insight into AI's reasoning, XAI builds trust, facilitates collaboration, and ensures accountability—key components of responsible AI.

The Road Ahead

Machine learning is the foundation of modern AI systems. From personalized recommendations on streaming platforms to self-driving cars navigating complex streets, ML enables machines to learn, adapt, and improve over time.

But as AI becomes more embedded in our lives, the focus must shift from mere performance to transparency and trust. In the next chapter, we'll dive deeper into neural networks— the architecture behind today's most advanced AI—and explore how they work, why they succeed, and the challenges they present for explainability.

Chapter 3

Inside the Neural Network

Brains of Silicon

From Neurons to Networks

The human brain is often described as the most complex system in the known universe. With billions of neurons, each connected to thousands of others, it enables us to perceive, reason, and act. Inspired by this biological marvel, researchers in the 1940s began to ask: could machines be designed to work in a similar way?

In 1943, Warren McCulloch and Walter Pitts introduced the first mathematical model of an artificial neuron. Their work laid the foundation for what would eventually become artificial neural networks. An artificial neuron receives input, processes it through a simple mathematical function, and produces an output. It's a basic decision-making unit: taking information, weighing its importance, and deciding whether to pass it along.

Individually, artificial neurons are simplistic. But when connected in networks, they become powerful tools capable of recognizing patterns and making decisions.

Anatomy of a Neural Network

A neural network is a layered system of artificial neurons. Information flows from the **input layer**, through one or more **hidden layers**, and ultimately to the **output layer**.

- **Input Layer**: The starting point where data enters the network—this could be the pixels from an image, words from a document, or numerical values from a spreadsheet.
- **Hidden Layers**: These layers transform the input data into useful representations. As information passes through each layer, the network learns increasingly abstract and complex features.
- **Output Layer**: The end result of the computation, such as predicting a category label or outputting a numerical score.

Connections between neurons carry **weights**, which control the strength of the signals being transmitted. Each neuron also includes a **bias**, which shifts the activation function's output. By adjusting these weights and biases, the network learns to map inputs to outputs—effectively generalizing from its training data to make predictions on new, unseen examples.

How Neural Networks Learn

The learning process in a neural network is called **training**. During training, the network makes predictions and compares them to the correct answers.

The difference between its prediction and the actual answer is measured by a **loss function**—essentially a score that indicates how far off the network's prediction was.

To improve its accuracy, the network adjusts its internal parameters using an algorithm called **backpropagation**. The process works as follows:

1. The network makes a prediction.
2. The loss function calculates the error.
3. The error is propagated backward through the network.
4. Weights and biases are adjusted to minimize future error.

This process is repeated across thousands, sometimes millions, of examples. Over time, the network becomes better at making accurate predictions.

A simple analogy is learning to throw a dart at a target. Each time you throw, you see where the dart lands. If you miss the bullseye, you adjust your aim based on feedback from your previous throws. Similarly, a neural network adjusts its parameters based on the feedback it receives from the loss function, gradually improving its aim.

Training relies on an optimization technique called **gradient descent**, which helps the network find the combination of weights and biases that minimize the loss. Imagine hiking down a mountain in search of the lowest point in the valley. Gradient descent guides the network step by step toward the optimal solution.

Deep Learning: Why Deeper is Better (and Sometimes Worse)

A **deep neural network** has many hidden layers. Adding layers allows the network to learn more complex and hierarchical patterns. For instance, in an image recognition system:

- Early layers detect simple features like edges and corners.
- Middle layers recognize shapes and textures.
- Deeper layers identify high-level structures, like objects and faces.

However, deeper networks are not without challenges:

- **Overfitting**: A deep network may perform exceptionally well on training data but poorly on new data because it has learned to memorize rather than generalize.
- **Vanishing Gradients**: In very deep networks, early layers can struggle to receive useful learning signals

during backpropagation, making them slow or ineffective at learning.

- **Data Hunger**: Deep networks require vast amounts of labeled data to train effectively.

Despite these challenges, deep learning has unlocked unprecedented capabilities in AI systems.

Neural Networks in Action

Neural networks are at the heart of many of today's most powerful AI applications.

1) Computer Vision

Convolutional Neural Networks (CNNs) have revolutionized computer vision. They excel at processing and interpreting images by recognizing patterns within small regions and combining them to form complex representations. CNNs power facial recognition systems, object detection in self-driving cars, and tumor identification in medical imaging.

2) Speech Recognition

Recurrent Neural Networks (RNNs) and their advanced form, **Long Short-Term Memory (LSTM)** networks, handle sequential data, making them ideal for speech recognition. They enable systems like Siri, Alexa, and Google Assistant to interpret and respond to spoken commands.

3) Natural Language Processing (NLP)

Neural networks have transformed NLP. Early models relied on RNNs, but modern systems use **transformers**, which we'll explore in the next chapter. These networks handle tasks like language translation, sentiment analysis, and text generation.

Case Study: How CNNs Help Machines "See"

Consider an airport security system using facial recognition to verify passengers' identities. A CNN processes the captured image, identifying key facial landmarks: distances between the eyes, shape of the nose, contour of the chin. These features are converted into a numerical representation—called an embedding—that is compared against a database.

Such systems have dramatically improved efficiency and security. Yet they raise ethical concerns about accuracy, particularly across diverse populations. Misidentification risks reinforce the need for explainable and fair AI systems, where decisions can be scrutinized and improved

---

Explainability in Deep Learning

Deep neural networks are often described as **black boxes** because their complex, multi-layered decision-making processes are difficult to interpret.

Efforts to improve transparency include:

- **Saliency Maps**: Visual tools that highlight which parts of an input (e.g., pixels in an image) influenced a model's decision.
- **Feature Importance Scores**: Techniques like **SHAP** and **LIME** that explain which factors were most significant in making a prediction.

Explainability isn't just about satisfying curiosity—it's about ensuring fairness, reducing bias, and building trust. For example, if an AI denies a loan application, the applicant and lender deserve to understand why. Was it due to income level, credit history, or another factor? Explainable AI makes such insights possible.

In healthcare, explainability helps doctors understand AI recommendations for diagnoses or treatments. When patients' lives are at stake, trust is paramount.

Looking Ahead: Neural Networks as the Foundation of Modern AI

Neural networks are the bedrock of modern AI. They power everything from voice assistants to self-driving cars, and their applications continue to expand.

But as AI systems grow more capable, the need for transparency, fairness, and explainability becomes more pressing.

As we look forward, advanced architectures like **transformers** are pushing the boundaries of what AI can achieve.

In the next chapter, we'll explore the transformer architecture—the engine behind breakthroughs in natural language understanding, and the foundation for models like GPT and BERT.

Chapter 4

Transformers

The Engines Powering Modern AI

From Recurrent Networks to Transformers: Why Change Was Needed

For years, Recurrent Neural Networks (RNNs) and their advanced versions, Long Short-Term Memory networks (LSTMs), were the backbone of AI systems dealing with sequential data. They powered speech recognition, language translation, and time-series predictions. However, these architectures had notable limitations. RNNs processed information sequentially, making them slow to train and inefficient at handling long-range dependencies—when understanding one part of a sequence depended on information far earlier in the input.

As sequences grew longer, RNNs struggled to retain context. For example, in a paragraph where the beginning sets the stage for the conclusion, an RNN might forget the earlier details by the time it reached the end. LSTMs mitigated this problem to some extent, but they were still constrained by their sequential nature and limited memory capacity.

The AI community needed an architecture that could process data more efficiently, with better scalability and the ability to handle long-term dependencies. In 2017, researchers at Google introduced a groundbreaking solution: the Transformer. It fundamentally changed how machines process sequential data by replacing recurrence with an attention-based mechanism, enabling parallel processing and vastly improving efficiency.

The Core Idea: Attention Is All You Need

The Transformer architecture was introduced in the paper titled *Attention Is All You Need*. Its core innovation was the **attention mechanism**, a method that allows a model to focus on the most relevant parts of the input, no matter their position in the sequence. This was a radical departure from previous architectures, which relied on step-by-step processing.

Imagine reading a complex document. Rather than reading every word sequentially, you might skim and focus on key phrases or headings to understand the gist. Similarly, the attention mechanism helps AI models weigh the importance of different words or tokens in a sequence, assigning greater focus to those most relevant for a given task. This approach not only improved learning efficiency but also enabled models to process data in parallel, dramatically speeding up training.

Self-Attention: Learning Context Relationships

At the heart of Transformers is **self-attention**, a mechanism that allows each word in an input to consider every other word when forming its representation. For instance, in the sentence, "The cat sat on the mat because it was tired," the model needs to understand that "it" refers to "the cat."

Self-attention makes this possible by enabling the network to directly link "it" with "the cat."

This capacity to model relationships regardless of distance makes Transformers uniquely powerful for understanding complex language and context.

How Transformers Work (Simplified)

The Transformer consists of two main components: the **encoder** and the **decoder**. For many tasks—especially in language modeling—only the encoder or decoder is used, but the full architecture includes both.

Encoder

The encoder processes the input data and generates a representation (embedding) that captures its meaning. It consists of multiple layers, each containing two key parts:

- **Multi-Head Self-Attention**: The model applies self-attention multiple times in parallel to capture different aspects of relationships between words.
- **Feedforward Neural Network**: A standard neural network that processes the attention output further.

Decoder

The decoder generates the output based on the encoder's representation. It also uses multi-head attention, but with an added mechanism to ensure it generates tokens sequentially, one at a time.

Positional Encoding

Unlike RNNs, Transformers process the entire input at once. This parallel processing requires a way to capture the order of tokens in a sequence. **Positional encoding** provides each token with information about its position, ensuring the model understands word order—a critical factor in language comprehension.

Why Transformers Are So Powerful

Transformers offer several advantages that have made them the architecture of choice for modern AI:

- **Parallel Processing**: Unlike RNNs, which process data sequentially, Transformers handle entire sequences simultaneously. This massively reduces training times and increases efficiency.
- **Scalability**: Transformers can be scaled to billions (and even trillions) of parameters and trained on vast datasets. This scalability enabled the creation of models like GPT-3, capable of generating human-like text and powering a new wave of AI applications.
- **Long-Range Dependencies**: Self-attention allows Transformers to learn dependencies between distant elements in a sequence more effectively than previous models.

Beyond language, Transformers have been adapted for image processing (Vision Transformers), biological data analysis (such as protein folding in AlphaFold), and even multimodal AI systems that handle text, images, and audio together.

Case Study: GPT, BERT, and the Language Models That Changed AI

GPT (Generative Pre-trained Transformer)

GPT models use a decoder-only Transformer architecture to generate coherent and contextually appropriate text. They are trained on massive amounts of internet data and fine-tuned for specific tasks. GPT-3, with 175 billion parameters, demonstrated the power of Transformers by producing human-like text and enabling chatbots, content creation tools, and code generation systems.

BERT (Bidirectional Encoder Representations from Transformers)

BERT introduced a new way to understand language by processing text in both directions—left-to-right and right-to-left—simultaneously. This bidirectional approach allows BERT to grasp the full context of a word based on its surrounding words, making it highly effective for tasks like search engine queries, sentiment analysis, and question answering.

Real-World Applications

Transformers power a wide range of applications:

- Chatbots that can engage in human-like conversation
- Automated translation services
- Content generation and summarization

- Search engines that deliver better, context-aware results
- AI-powered customer support tools

Explainability and Challenges in Transformers

While Transformers are powerful, they are not without challenges.

Interpretability

Attention mechanisms offer some insights into how a model makes decisions—attention weights can indicate which parts of an input were most influential. However, researchers caution that attention scores don't always provide a full explanation of the model's reasoning. Additional techniques, like SHAP and LIME, are often needed to understand the complex decisions of large Transformer models.

Ethical Concerns

Transformers are trained on enormous datasets collected from the internet, which may contain biases. Without careful oversight, these biases can be amplified in the models' outputs, leading to ethical concerns such as reinforcing stereotypes or misinformation. AI researchers and organizations are increasingly adopting dataset curation practices and bias detection tools to mitigate these risks.

Computational Costs and Environmental Impact

Training large Transformer models consumes vast amounts of computational resources and energy, raising concerns about their environmental impact. Efforts are underway to develop more efficient models and training methods to reduce this footprint.

Looking Ahead: Multimodal AI and the Future beyond Transformers

Transformers are evolving beyond text to handle multiple types of data simultaneously:

- **Multimodal Transformers**: Models like OpenAI's CLIP and Google's Flamingo combine text, images, and audio, enabling them to understand and generate complex multimedia content.

- **Transformers in Biology**: DeepMind's AlphaFold uses Transformer-like architectures to predict protein structures, revolutionizing molecular biology and drug discovery.

As models like GPT-4 continue to push the boundaries of AI, researchers are exploring new architectures and techniques to make Transformers more efficient, interpretable, and responsible.

Next: Deploying AI in the Real World

In the next chapter, we'll explore how AI systems are deployed in practical settings—moving from powerful models to real-world applications that shape industries and everyday life.

The Blueprint of Artificial Intelligence in Practice

Part II

Inside AI Systems

How Machines Learn and Work

Chapter 5

Deploying AI in the Real World

From Lab Models to Everyday Applications

From Concept to Reality: Deploying AI Systems

The journey of artificial intelligence does not end with developing an accurate model in the controlled environment of a lab. In many ways, that's just the beginning. Moving AI from research prototypes to real-world systems requires a rigorous process of deployment, integration, and ongoing management. Deployment is where AI begins to create tangible value—impacting businesses, healthcare, transportation, and society at large.

But the real world is messy. Data streams are inconsistent, environments unpredictable, and user expectations high. Successfully deploying AI requires robust systems, ethical considerations, and an understanding of operational challenges that go far beyond training a high-performing model.

Building the Foundation: Data Pipelines and Infrastructure

For AI to function reliably in production, it must be fed with high-quality, timely data. Data pipelines are the arteries of an AI system, ensuring that raw data flows seamlessly from sources—like sensors, apps, or user interactions—through cleaning, transformation, and into the AI model.

- **Data Ingestion**: Gathering data from various sources—structured and unstructured.
- **Data Processing**: Cleaning, normalizing, and validating data to ensure quality.
- **Data Delivery**: Pushing processed data to AI models in real-time (streaming) or in batches.

Case Study: Netflix

Netflix's recommendation engine relies on a sophisticated data pipeline. Every user action—pauses, rewinds, searches—is captured and processed in real-time. Their AI models continuously update personalized recommendations, balancing speed, privacy, and accuracy for millions of users across the globe.

AI at Scale: Cloud and Edge Deployment

Scaling AI for widespread use requires robust infrastructure. Two primary approaches have emerged: **cloud deployment** and **edge deployment**.

- **Cloud AI**: Cloud platforms (AWS, Azure, Google Cloud) offer flexibility and computing power, allowing businesses to deploy AI models as APIs and services. It simplifies updates and maintenance while supporting massive data processing.
- **Edge AI**: AI models are deployed directly on local devices (smartphones, drones, autonomous vehicles). This minimizes latency and enhances privacy since data doesn't need to be sent to the cloud. However, edge AI is limited by local hardware constraints.

Example: Self-Driving Cars

Autonomous vehicles rely on edge AI for real-time decisions—recognizing pedestrians, detecting obstacles, and adjusting routes instantly. Processing must occur on-board, where speed and reliability are critical.

AI in Action: Real-World Industry Applications

AI is transforming industries by automating processes, uncovering insights, and delivering personalized experiences.

Healthcare

AI assists clinicians in diagnosis, treatment planning, and patient monitoring. Computer vision models analyze medical images to detect diseases like cancer and diabetic retinopathy earlier and more accurately.

Case Study: IBM Watson Health

Watson promised to revolutionize oncology treatment recommendations. While its initial potential was impressive, real-world challenges arose—data integration issues, clinician trust, and inconsistent outcomes. This case underscores the complexity of deploying AI in critical, high-stakes fields.

Finance

AI enhances fraud detection by analyzing transaction patterns in real time. Machine learning models assess creditworthiness, automate trading, and detect anomalies that may indicate fraud.

Retail and E-Commerce

Recommendation engines use AI to personalize product suggestions, improving user engagement and boosting sales. AI-driven inventory management predicts demand and optimizes supply chains, while chatbots streamline customer service.

Transportation and Logistics

AI powers route optimization for delivery services and autonomous vehicles. Logistics companies like FedEx and UPS use AI to predict package delays, optimize routes, and reduce fuel consumption.

From Deployment to Maintenance: Monitoring AI in Production

Deployment isn't the final step. AI systems need continuous monitoring and maintenance to remain accurate and ethical.

Model Drift

AI models degrade over time as real-world data shifts. A customer churn model trained on last year's data may become less effective as market dynamics evolve. Detecting **model drift** requires ongoing evaluation and periodic retraining.

Continuous Learning

Some systems adopt **continuous learning**, where AI models adapt by incorporating new data regularly. This approach demands careful monitoring to prevent unintended behaviors or biases from creeping in.

Governance and Auditing

AI systems must undergo regular audits to ensure they comply with ethical and legal standards. Governance frameworks are essential for maintaining transparency, fairness, and accountability in AI decision-making.

Explainable AI: Opening the Black Box

Explainability is no longer optional in many industries—it's a necessity. Stakeholders need to understand why AI systems make specific decisions, especially when outcomes impact health, finances, or personal freedoms.

Tools for Explainable AI:

- **Saliency Maps**: Visual explanations highlighting which parts of an input (image or text) influenced a decision.
- **SHAP and LIME**: Techniques that assign importance scores to features, showing which variables had the greatest influence.

Case Study: Healthcare Diagnostics
In radiology, AI models that flag suspicious areas in medical scans must provide reasons clinicians can trust. Saliency maps help highlight why the model focuses on certain areas, enabling doctors to validate or question the AI's recommendations.

Explainability builds trust, promotes responsible use, and ensures regulatory compliance in sectors where AI decisions carry significant weight.

Risks and Ethical Considerations in AI Deployment

AI systems in production face complex challenges beyond performance metrics.

Security and Adversarial Attacks

Malicious actors can manipulate AI systems using adversarial examples—subtly altered data that tricks models into making incorrect predictions. Defending against such attacks requires robust testing and resilience measures.

Privacy and Data Protection

AI relies on vast datasets, often containing sensitive personal information. Compliance with regulations like GDPR and HIPAA is essential. Techniques like **differential privacy** and **federated learning** help protect user data.

Bias and Fairness

Biases in training data can perpetuate discrimination in AI decisions—denying loans, targeting ads unfairly, or skewing criminal risk assessments. Ethical AI frameworks and fairness audits help identify and mitigate these issues before they harm real users.

The Future of AI Deployment: AI as Critical Infrastructure

As AI becomes embedded in everyday life, it is evolving into essential infrastructure. AI optimizes energy grids, predicts equipment failures in manufacturing, and enhances agricultural yields with precision farming.

The next phase of AI deployment involves **human-in-the-loop** systems that combine AI efficiency with human judgment—particularly for high-stakes decisions like medical diagnoses or autonomous driving.

Ethical deployment of AI requires transparency, accountability, and careful governance. As we move toward more autonomous AI systems, ensuring that they operate safely and fairly will be an ongoing responsibility.

What's Next: Explainable AI in Focus

In the next chapter, we will take a deeper dive into **Explainable AI (XAI)**—exploring the methods, tools, and principles that make AI systems more transparent, trustworthy, and accountable.

Chapter 6: Explainable AI

Opening the Black Box

Why Explainability Matters

As artificial intelligence systems become more powerful and more integrated into our lives, understanding *how* they make decisions becomes increasingly important. Whether it's a loan approval algorithm, a medical diagnosis tool, or an AI assistant helping a judge assess bail risk, the decisions made by machines can affect someone's health, financial future, or personal freedom.

But trust isn't built on accuracy alone. Even highly accurate models can be viewed with suspicion if they can't explain their reasoning. This is the core of the explainability challenge: when AI acts as a black box, trust, fairness, and accountability are all at risk.

What Is Explainable AI?

Explainable AI (XAI) refers to methods and tools that make AI systems' decision-making processes understandable to humans. It's a broad concept that includes:

- **Interpretability**: How well a human can comprehend the internal mechanics of the model.

- **Transparency**: Whether the system's structure and inputs are open to inspection.
- **Explainability**: The ability of the system to produce understandable justifications for its outputs.

Some models, like decision trees or linear regression, are inherently interpretable. Others—particularly deep neural networks—require post-hoc explanations to clarify their decisions. Regulations like the EU's GDPR include a "right to explanation," highlighting how legal frameworks are beginning to demand explainability in AI.

In regulated industries like banking and insurance, simpler, interpretable models are often favored over black-box solutions—even at the cost of some accuracy—because they are easier to audit and justify.

Techniques for Explaining AI

There is no one-size-fits-all method for explainability. Instead, researchers have developed a toolkit of techniques, suited to different models and contexts.

For Simpler Models

- **Decision Trees**: Their if-then logic makes decisions easy to follow.
- **Linear and Logistic Regression**: The contribution of each variable is directly visible in the model's coefficients.

These models are preferred where transparency is essential to meet legal or organizational standards.

For Complex Models

When working with models like deep neural networks, more sophisticated explanation methods are needed:

- **LIME (Local Interpretable Model-Agnostic Explanations)**: LIME explains individual predictions by approximating the complex model locally with a simpler one. It's especially useful for surfacing the logic behind specific outputs. However, LIME can sometimes produce inconsistent results, especially when the input space is high-dimensional or sensitive to sampling noise.
- **SHAP (SHapley Additive exPlanations)**: SHAP uses game theory to assign each feature a contribution score, offering a globally consistent way to interpret model behavior.
- **Saliency Maps and Grad-CAM**: Used in computer vision, these techniques highlight the parts of an image that most influenced the model's prediction.
- **Attention Visualization**: In transformer-based models, attention scores can sometimes help identify which input elements were most important for a decision.

Case Study: Explainability in Healthcare AI

Imagine a radiology AI system designed to detect lung cancer in CT scans. A model flags a region of concern. But how does a doctor know the model is reliable? What if it's reacting to noise in the image or an unrelated artifact?

Here, explainability is essential. A saliency map that visually highlights the exact region the AI used in its assessment allows the doctor to evaluate the machine's decision critically. If the highlighted region matches the area a trained radiologist would have focused on, trust in the system increases.

Explainability doesn't just reassure users—it facilitates collaboration between humans and machines.

Challenges in Explainable AI

While XAI is essential, it is far from straightforward.

Simplified Doesn't Mean Accurate

Explanations are, by nature, simplifications. A risk arises when simplified explanations distort the true logic of a model. For instance, a loan approval model may use location data as a proxy for socioeconomic status—something ethically problematic—but the explanation might highlight seemingly neutral features instead. Users may overtrust or misunderstand the explanation, believing it represents the entire decision-making process.

The Trade-off: Accuracy vs. Interpretability

There's often a tension between model complexity and interpretability. Simpler models are easier to understand but may lack the predictive power of complex architectures like deep neural networks. Choosing between them involves weighing transparency against performance.

Overtrusting the Explanation

Sometimes, people place too much confidence in an explanation simply because it *feels* right. Cognitive biases— like confirmation bias—can lead users to accept incorrect or misleading model behavior.

The Human Side of Explainability

Effective explanations aren't one-size-fits-all. What a data scientist finds useful may overwhelm a policymaker or confuse a customer.

Explainability should be **audience-aware**:

- For developers: granular, technical explanations aid debugging and refinement.
- For end-users: concise, intuitive justifications build trust and understanding.

- For regulators: documentation and transparency
- Ensure legal compliance.

The challenge lies in designing explanations that satisfy all of these audiences without oversimplifying or overcomplicating the underlying model. This is where **human-in-the-loop** systems—where humans oversee and validate AI outputs— play a crucial role in ensuring explainable AI is truly useful.

The Road Ahead for XAI

Explainable AI is a rapidly evolving field. New techniques are emerging to provide richer, more faithful, and more user-centric explanations. Areas of future growth include:

- **Counterfactual Explanations**: Showing how a small change in input (e.g., a slightly higher income) could have led to a different outcome (e.g., loan approval).
- **Causal Reasoning**: Moving beyond correlations to explain *why* outcomes happen.
- **Interactive Explanations**: Letting users explore and query AI decisions dynamically.

Explainability is also becoming a core component of **ethical AI** frameworks. As AI influences more decisions—from healthcare and finance to hiring and justice—transparency will be critical to ensuring fairness, accountability, and public trust.

In the next chapter, we'll explore the ethical dimensions of AI more fully, including fairness, bias, responsibility, and the societal implications of intelligent machines.

Chapter 7

Ethical Intelligence

Fairness, Responsibility, and the Future of AI

Why Ethics in AI Matters

Artificial intelligence is no longer a futuristic concept—it is an active participant in society. From hiring decisions to medical diagnoses to predictive policing, AI systems are making or influencing decisions that directly affect people's lives. With this power comes an urgent question: how do we ensure AI behaves ethically?

When AI systems make mistakes, the consequences can be severe. Biased hiring algorithms can reinforce discrimination. Facial recognition can misidentify individuals, especially from marginalized communities. An AI used to recommend bail or parole decisions may carry hidden systemic bias. These real-world failures remind us that building intelligent systems isn't just a technical challenge—it's a moral one.

Ethical AI isn't about perfection; it's about responsibility. It's about designing systems that are fair, accountable, and aligned with human values.

The Dimensions of AI Ethics

AI ethics is a broad and evolving field, but it can be organized into several key dimensions:

- **Fairness**: AI systems should not discriminate based on race, gender, age, or other protected attributes. Fairness means correcting historical imbalances and ensuring equitable outcomes.
- **Accountability**: Who is responsible when AI makes a harmful decision? Developers, deployers, and regulators must all share accountability. There must be clear lines of responsibility.
- **Transparency**: Users and stakeholders must understand how AI systems make decisions. This requires openness about data sources, model design, and limitations.
- **Privacy**: AI systems often rely on large datasets that include sensitive personal information. Protecting that data—and ensuring it is used with consent—is essential.
- **Autonomy**: AI should empower rather than replace human decision-making. Especially in critical areas like medicine or criminal justice, the final judgment should remain with a human.

Understanding Bias in AI

Bias is one of the most pressing ethical challenges in AI. It can creep in at multiple points:

- **Biased data**: If training data reflects historical prejudices, AI will learn and perpetuate them.
- **Biased models**: Even with balanced data, the way models are constructed or evaluated can introduce bias.
- **Biased outcomes**: The results of AI systems may impact certain groups unfairly, reinforcing inequality.

Case Study: Amazon's Hiring Algorithm

In an effort to automate recruiting, Amazon trained an AI model on resumes from previous hires—most of whom were men. The model learned to downgrade resumes that included words like "women's chess club" or came from women's colleges. It had absorbed the bias of historical hiring patterns.

Case Study: Healthcare Risk Scores (Optum)

A U.S. healthcare algorithm designed to identify high-risk patients used healthcare spending as a proxy. Because Black patients historically had less access to care, the model underestimated their risk, leading to unequal treatment and care.

Bias Auditing Tools: Open-source libraries like **Fairlearn, Aequitas**, and **IBM AI Fairness 360** are helping teams measure and mitigate bias. Metrics like **equalized odds** and **demographic parity** guide fair model evaluation.

Human Oversight and Accountability

AI systems don't exist in isolation—they are built, deployed, and monitored by humans. Accountability begins with recognizing that no AI decision is truly autonomous.

Human-in-the-loop systems ensure that critical decisions always involve a human reviewer. In medicine, for example, an AI may suggest a diagnosis, but a doctor should always validate the recommendation.

Case Study: Criminal Justice and COMPAS

Some U.S. courts have used COMPAS, an AI system predicting recidivism, to guide bail and sentencing decisions. Investigations found that the tool was biased against Black defendants, flagging them as higher risk more often than white counterparts. Yet, when mistakes occurred, responsibility was murky—was it the court, the developers, or the software company?

This underscores a vital point: accountability must be embedded in every layer of the AI lifecycle.

Ethical Frameworks and Guidelines

Numerous organizations have developed ethical principles to guide AI development and deployment:

- **OECD and UNESCO**: Emphasize human rights, fairness, transparency, and robustness.
- **European Commission**: Introduced the High-Level Expert Group on AI, outlining seven key requirements for trustworthy AI.
- **Companies and Consortia**: Google, Microsoft, and OpenAI have published internal AI principles and created ethics boards—though with mixed results and controversies.

Quote: "Fairness is not just a technical problem—it's a social one." — Timnit Gebru, AI ethicist

While these frameworks signal progress, implementation often lags. Ethics must be embedded in design and workflow—not just declared in public statements.

Governance, Regulation, and the Law

As AI becomes more powerful, regulation is following.

- **GDPR** in Europe guarantees a right to explanation, data protection, and consent.
- The **EU AI Act** proposes a risk-based framework, regulating AI based on potential harm.
- In the U.S., proposed legislation like the **Algorithmic Accountability Act** would require audits and transparency for high-risk systems.

Legal personhood for AI—a topic once confined to sci-fi—is now debated in policy circles. Most ethicists argue that ultimate responsibility must remain with human actors.

Cultural and Global Perspectives

Ethics is not one-size-fits-all. Cultural values influence how we prioritize fairness, privacy, and autonomy.

Voice assistants often struggle with accents from India, Nigeria, or Jamaica—an example of how AI trained predominantly on Western voices excludes many users.

In Indigenous communities, data is often seen as communal rather than individual. Western AI systems built around individual consent models may clash with these values.

We must develop **inclusive AI** that accounts for linguistic, cultural, and socioeconomic diversity. Equitable AI means *localizing ethics*, not imposing a single vision.

Looking Ahead: Toward Ethical and Human-Centered AI

The path forward lies in designing AI that amplifies human values. That means building systems that are transparent, fair, and inclusive by design—not by afterthought.

AI for Social Good initiatives are already paving the way:

- AI predicting wildfires to enable early evacuation
- Natural language models helping Indigenous communities preserve endangered languages
- Crop analytics tools supporting smallholder farmers in Africa and Southeast Asia

Ethical AI also means *who gets to participate* in building it. Diverse teams build better, fairer systems. Communities must have a voice in the technologies deployed in their lives.

Quote: "We need to stop treating ethics like a bolt-on. It must be baked into the system." — Margaret Mitchell

The future of AI isn't just about intelligence. It's about empathy, justice, and shared progress. As we move toward an age of increasingly autonomous systems, we must ask not just, *can* machines decide—but *should* they?

In the final part of this book, we'll look to the horizon—exploring the evolving frontiers of AI, the dream of general intelligence, and the promise of a human-AI partnership grounded in trust.

Exploring the Frontiers of Intelligence, Creativity, and Human-AI Possibilities

Part III

AI Tomorrow

Imagination, Innovation, and the Unknown

Chapter 8

The Next Wave

Frontiers in AI Research

Beyond What We Know

Artificial intelligence has come a long way—from rule-based systems and neural networks to transformers and large language models. Yet as powerful as today's systems are, they are still limited in scope, generalization, and understanding. The next wave of AI research seeks to address these limitations while pushing the boundaries of what machines can do.

In this chapter, we explore what's on the research horizon: from the evolution of foundational models and learning paradigms to cross-disciplinary breakthroughs and the pursuit of broader, more adaptive forms of intelligence.

From Narrow to Broad: The Generalization Challenge

Most current AI systems are trained for narrow tasks. A system that excels at identifying objects in images can't necessarily write poetry, navigate traffic, or plan a business strategy. Even the most sophisticated large language models

63

lack true reasoning, grounded understanding, or flexibility across diverse domains.

The next wave in AI is focused on **generalization**—creating systems that can adapt to new tasks with minimal retraining, understand abstract concepts, and learn from fewer examples.

Self-supervised learning is a major area of growth. Instead of relying on labeled data, models learn by predicting parts of data from other parts—just as children learn language by listening and guessing meaning from context. This method has driven much of the progress behind language models like BERT and GPT.

Case Study: Meta's DINOv2
Meta's DINOv2 (Self-Distillation with No Labels) is a self-supervised vision transformer trained without any human-labeled data. It achieves near state-of-the-art performance in object classification, segmentation, and detection. Its significance lies not just in performance, but in demonstrating that high-quality visual representations can be learned without expensive, manual annotation—opening doors to more inclusive and scalable AI systems.

Another approach is **meta-learning**, or "learning to learn." These systems aim to understand the structure of tasks so they can generalize more quickly. They don't just memorize data—they adapt across new challenges.

Foundation Models and Scaling Laws

One of the most important developments in recent years is the rise of **foundation models**—massive, versatile models trained on broad data at scale, and then fine-tuned for specific tasks. GPT, PaLM, and LLaMA are examples. These models exhibit **emergent behaviors**—capabilities that appear suddenly when model size crosses certain thresholds.

Researchers are studying **scaling laws**: mathematical relationships that predict how model performance improves with more data, compute, and parameters. For instance, a doubling of model size or dataset size often yields a predictable improvement in accuracy or reduction in loss— until the law breaks down due to other constraints. Understanding these laws helps guide future architecture design and resource allocation.

Case Study: OpenAI's GPT-4
GPT-4 is a large multimodal foundation model that exhibits surprising levels of reasoning, instruction-following, and creativity. Despite not being explicitly trained for many of its capabilities, GPT-4 can solve complex problems in math, law, and language, exemplifying the unpredictable emergent properties of scaled systems. Its growing utility also raises new questions about safety, explainability, and control.

Still, foundation models come with limitations. They're expensive to train, prone to hallucinations, and difficult to control. The next wave of research is focused on improving efficiency, **robustness**, and **alignment**—ensuring AI systems do what we intend, safely and reliably.

Neurosymbolic AI: Blending Logic with Learning

Deep learning excels at pattern recognition but struggles with abstract reasoning. In contrast, symbolic AI—based on logic, rules, and structure—offers interpretability but lacks adaptability.

Neurosymbolic AI combines the two. These hybrid systems use neural networks for perception and statistical learning, while incorporating symbolic reasoning for structure and logic. This could lead to AI that not only sees and predicts—but understands and explains.

Case Study: IBM's Project Debater

IBM's Project Debater was an early exploration of combining structured argument models (symbolic) with natural language processing and retrieval (neural). It could formulate coherent arguments, rebut counterpoints, and synthesize supporting evidence. While not flawless in debate performance, it demonstrated the promise of integrating symbolic structure with statistical fluency—paving the way for more reasoned and interpretable AI.

A neurosymbolic system in medical diagnosis might analyze scans using deep learning, then reason about symptoms and treatment pathways using a rule-based expert system. This blend improves accuracy and interpretability.

AI in Science: Discovery Accelerators

AI is becoming a powerful tool in scientific discovery. In biology, **AlphaFold** has revolutionized protein structure prediction—solving a problem that baffled scientists for decades.

Case Study: DeepMind's AlphaFold

AlphaFold predicted the 3D structure of proteins with near-laboratory accuracy. It unlocked insights into how biological systems function, aiding drug development, genomics, and molecular biology. When AlphaFold's predictions for nearly every known protein structure were released freely to the scientific community, it marked not only a breakthrough in biology but a milestone in collaborative, open science.

In climate science, AI models help simulate complex systems and predict weather patterns. In materials science, generative models explore the chemical space for new molecules and materials.

Case Study: Nvidia's FourCastNet

Nvidia's FourCastNet is an AI-powered weather prediction system that can generate forecasts faster and with greater resolution than traditional methods. By learning from satellite and climate data, it helps scientists better anticipate extreme weather and study climate change scenarios—enhancing both disaster preparedness and environmental research.

The rise of **scientific AI agents**—models fine-tuned for hypothesis generation, data analysis, and experimentation—hints at a future where machines become collaborators in research, accelerating discovery across disciplines.

Challenges and the Unknowns Ahead

As research pushes forward, big questions remain:

- How far can scale take us? Are we approaching diminishing returns?
- Can we build AI systems that reason, not just predict?
- How do we evaluate emerging capabilities we didn't explicitly train for?
- Can we design models that are energy-efficient, robust, and safe by default?

We are entering a phase where the questions are no longer just technical, but philosophical. What kind of intelligence do we truly want to create? What values should guide that creation? And what role will humans play in a world increasingly shaped by thinking machines?

In the next chapter, we'll explore a different frontier—AI that senses, moves, and interacts with the world: **multimodal and embodied AI**.

Chapter 9

Multimodal and Embodied AI

Sensing the World beyond Text: Toward Sensory Intelligence

Artificial intelligence has achieved remarkable progress in understanding language, recognizing images, and making decisions. Yet, these achievements often occur in silos—vision, language, and sound processed separately by specialized models. In contrast, human perception is inherently multimodal: we don't just read or see, we experience the world through a rich blend of senses and embodied movement.

To build more human-like and capable systems, researchers are now developing **multimodal** and **embodied AI**—technologies that can integrate visual, linguistic, auditory, and tactile information, and act in the physical world. This chapter explores how machines are learning to sense, interpret, and move through the world, bridging the gap between abstract intelligence and grounded experience.

What Is Multimodal AI?

Multimodal AI refers to systems that can process and understand more than one type of data at a time—text, images, video, audio, and more. This integration allows machines to interpret complex real-world scenarios more effectively.

For instance, when you describe a photograph, you're interpreting visual elements through language. A multimodal AI system performs a similar task—connecting pixels to words, sound waves to speech, or gestures to intent. The result is a machine that can generate captions, answer questions about images, or understand conversations in noisy environments.

Case Study: CLIP, Flamingo, and Gemini

CLIP (Contrastive Language–Image Pretraining), developed by OpenAI, connects images with textual descriptions. Trained on a massive dataset of image-caption pairs, CLIP can recognize objects, understand abstract visual concepts, and perform zero-shot learning—making predictions on tasks it was never directly trained on.

Flamingo, created by DeepMind, extends this capability by blending visual and textual reasoning. It can generate coherent answers to questions about images and video clips, showing early signs of fluid, multimodal intelligence.

Google's Gemini takes a further step by combining language, vision, and reasoning in a unified model. It can solve logic puzzles using diagrams, interpret charts, and answer queries about complex visual documents. These systems signal a shift from task-specific models to general-purpose perception engines.

Embodied AI: Machines That Move

While multimodal AI focuses on perception, **embodied AI** is about action—intelligent agents that physically interact with their surroundings. Embodied systems use sensors (cameras, microphones, touch sensors) and actuators (arms, wheels, legs) to perceive, plan, and execute real-world behaviors.

Unlike software-only models, embodied agents must handle uncertainty, noise, and constant environmental change. They need to learn from trial and error, understand cause and effect, and respond in real time.

Case Study: Boston Dynamics and Tesla Optimus

Boston Dynamics has become synonymous with agile, mobile robots. Its quadruped robot **Spot** can walk, climb stairs, and navigate hazardous environments. Meanwhile, **Atlas**, a bipedal robot, performs dynamic movements like parkour and backflips—thanks to a fusion of AI and control theory.

Tesla's Optimus project envisions general-purpose humanoid robots capable of assisting in factories or homes. Although early in development, Optimus combines AI perception, locomotion, and manipulation to move toward robots that can perform useful human tasks.

Case Study: SayCan and PaLM-E

Google's **SayCan** project connects a large language model (PaLM) with a robotic platform to follow verbal instructions like "bring me an apple." The robot reasons about which actions are possible, prioritizes them, and executes them in the real world.

PaLM-E, an evolution of this idea, integrates proprioception (awareness of one's own body), images, and language into a single large model. It allows robots to navigate, understand context, and adapt their actions—all while interpreting natural language input.

Sensing the World: Touch, Sound, and Shape

Beyond sight and speech, embodied AI also explores other senses:

- **Touch**: Tactile sensors help robots handle delicate objects. For instance, GelSight's high-resolution sensors give robots the ability to "feel" surface textures and pressure.

- **Sound**: Audio analysis enhances spatial awareness, emotion detection, and safety. Voice-commanded robots rely on auditory cues to interact with users.
- **Shape adaptation**: Projects like MIT's **RoboGrammar** and soft robotics explore how robots can design or morph their own structures based on terrain and tasks.

Example: In medical robotics, tactile AI enables minimally invasive procedures by detecting tissue resistance, improving both safety and accuracy.

Why Multimodal and Embodied AI Matters

Multimodal and embodied systems are not just cool—they're necessary for AI to function in the real world. Integrating perception with action enables:

- **Safer human-AI interaction**: Machines that understand tone, gesture, and environment can respond more intuitively.
- **More flexible functionality**: A robot that can listen, see, and act can adapt to changing environments and instructions.
- **Accessible AI**: Multimodal systems can assist users with different abilities—e.g., visual input for deaf users or voice output for the blind.

Ultimately, this branch of AI brings us closer to building systems that are aware, adaptive, and collaborative—capable not just of computing, but of coexisting.

Challenges and Reflections

Despite its promise, multimodal and embodied AI faces major challenges:

- **Training complexity**: Collecting and synchronizing multimodal data is resource-intensive.
- **Safety and trust**: Embodied agents operate in shared spaces with people. Robust safety protocols are essential.
- **Bias and generalization**: Perceptual systems must work across diverse settings and user populations.
- **Ethics**: As machines begin to resemble and interact with humans, questions arise about social cues, expectations, and emotional engagement.

Multimodal and embodied AI marks a turning point—where intelligence leaves the lab and enters the world. It demands not only technical innovation but ethical design, interdisciplinary thinking, and a deep respect for the human environments it inhabits.

In the next chapter, we'll explore how these intelligent systems are learning not just to sense and act—but to imagine, compose, and create.

Chapter 10

AI and Creativity

When Machines Imagine: Rethinking Creativity in the Age of Machines

For centuries, creativity—our ability to imagine, invent, and express—has been seen as uniquely human. Poetry, painting, music, storytelling—these were sacred spaces of the mind, untouched by code or computation. But today, artificial intelligence is stepping into the studio, the writer's room, and the symphony hall. And it's not just observing—it's creating.

AI systems can now compose music, generate artwork, write novels, and even invent new styles. But is this truly creativity, or simply an echo of human data? Are these machines artists—or tools trained to mimic? In this chapter, we explore how AI is reshaping creative expression, the technologies behind this shift, and the questions it raises about authorship, imagination, and the future of art.

Generative AI: Algorithms That Create

Generative AI refers to systems that produce new content—text, images, sound, or video—based on what they've learned from massive datasets. Powered by transformer architectures and trained on billions of examples, these models go beyond analysis—they generate.

From GPT-4 and DALL·E to Stable Diffusion and MusicLM, we now have tools that can write sonnets, sketch surreal cityscapes, compose ambient music, and design logos in seconds. These models don't "understand" in a human sense, but they excel at replicating form, style, and structure with uncanny fluency.

Case Study: GPT-4 and the Art of Storytelling

OpenAI's GPT-4 can draft essays, write poetry, mimic famous authors, and even construct multi-character dialogues. Writers use tools like **Sudowrite**, built on GPT, to brainstorm scenes, flesh out characters, or overcome writer's block.

Science fiction author Hugh Howey and other novelists have publicly shared how these tools serve as creative partners—offering suggestions, stylistic rewrites, or plot twists they hadn't considered. While AI lacks lived experience or true emotion, it can simulate the patterns of storytelling with impressive depth.

Case Study: Visual Art with DALL·E, Midjourney, and Stable Diffusion

Image generators transform words into visuals. A prompt like "a futuristic city at sunset, painted in watercolor" can yield a gallery of artworks in moments.

In 2022, **Théâtre D'opéra Spatial**, an image created using Midjourney by artist Jason Allen, won a state art competition in Colorado. The backlash was swift—had a human really created this? Should AI-generated works compete with human artists? The debate highlighted the growing tension between inspiration and automation.

Many visual artists now use AI as a conceptual partner— prototyping ideas, blending styles, or generating assets. But concerns remain around plagiarism, style mimicry, and fair attribution.

Case Study: Music by Machine—Aiva and MusicLM

AI is composing soundscapes as well. **Aiva**, an AI composer trained on classical scores, creates music for films, games, and commercials. It's even registered with music rights organizations, raising questions about legal ownership.

MusicLM, developed by Google, can generate tracks from prompts like "jazz saxophone solo with a melancholic mood." These systems let non-musicians prototype music ideas with minimal input.

While some musicians welcome these tools as collaborators, others fear a loss of originality or emotional depth. Can music composed without feeling still move us?

From Canvas to Keyboard: AI in Creative Workflows

Rather than replacing artists, many AI tools serve as co-creators:

- Writers use GPT to outline plots or rephrase clunky sentences.
- Designers use Adobe's **Firefly** and **Canva Magic Studio** to generate layouts and marketing visuals.
- Video editors use **Runway** to clean, color, and reimagine footage with AI-powered tools.

In these workflows, AI is a brush, not the hand that holds it. It accelerates iteration, expands possibilities, and democratizes design for creators with limited resources or training.

Case Study: Filmmaking with AI

Short films like *The Safe Zone* have been scripted with GPT-generated dialogue, storyboarded using DALL·E, and edited with AI-powered software. While these films still rely heavily on human direction and refinement, they reveal how AI is creeping into every corner of the creative pipeline.

This new model of storytelling—part human, part machine—challenges our assumptions about creativity as a purely organic process.

Can Machines Truly Be Creative?

The question lingers: is AI creative, or merely combinatorial?

Creativity is often defined by novelty, value, and intent. AI can generate novelty. It can produce work that we find valuable. But what about intent? Can a system without consciousness or emotion truly be said to "create"?

Some philosophers argue that creativity is in the eye of the beholder—if the output inspires, provokes, or moves us, perhaps the process is secondary. Others insist that creativity without awareness is imitation, not invention.

Either way, AI is forcing us to rethink what creativity really means—and who gets to claim it.

The Ethics of AI-Generated Art

With creativity comes controversy:

- **Attribution**: Should generative models credit the artists they learned from?
- **Ownership**: If a user enters a prompt and the AI renders an image, who owns it?
- **Bias**: Training data often reflects cultural, racial, and gender biases. Generated art can unintentionally reinforce stereotypes.
- **Displacement**: As AI becomes more capable, will it undercut livelihoods in writing, illustration, music, or design?

In 2023, **Getty Images** sued Stability AI for using its copyrighted content to train image models without permission. Legal frameworks are struggling to keep up with the rapid pace of generative technology.

Ethical AI art requires transparency, fairness, and safeguards. It's not just about what machines can make—but what kind of creative culture we want to shape together.

What Lies Ahead: The Future of Machine-Made Imagination

AI may never feel, but it can imagine—at least statistically. And as generative tools evolve, we may see:

- Interactive stories that adapt to your mood and choices
- Personalized music for every listener
- Augmented creativity across every medium
- Entirely new art forms born from human-AI fusion

Perhaps creativity is not diminished by AI—it is multiplied. Just as photography expanded painting, and sampling reshaped music, AI may open new dimensions of artistic possibility.

In the next chapter, we move from creativity to consciousness—into one of the most debated frontiers of AI: **Artificial General Intelligence.** Myth or momentum? Let's find out.

Chapter 11

Artificial General Intelligence

Myth or Momentum: Beyond Narrow Intelligence

Today's AI systems are powerful, but focused. They translate languages, label images, generate code, and pass exams—but only within the boundaries of tasks they've been trained on. This kind of **narrow intelligence** dominates the current landscape. These models are brilliant specialists, not generalists.

Artificial General Intelligence (AGI) represents a different vision entirely: machines that can think, reason, learn, and adapt across a wide range of tasks and contexts—just like humans. AGI wouldn't just follow instructions; it would set goals, solve problems, and even explore new domains without retraining.

Is AGI a matter of time, a leap of imagination, or a technological mirage? In this chapter, we explore what AGI is, who's building it, and how close—or far—we might be from making it real.

Defining General Intelligence

There's no strict definition of AGI, but common features include:

- **Transfer learning**: Applying knowledge from one task to another
- **Reasoning and planning**: Solving problems with logic, goals, and foresight
- **Autonomy**: Acting without hand-holding or narrow task definitions
- **Adaptation**: Learning and evolving in dynamic, unfamiliar environments

AGI is not about doing one thing brilliantly—it's about doing many things adequately, and improving through experience.

Case Study: Gato by DeepMind

DeepMind's **Gato** was trained to perform a range of tasks: playing games, navigating environments, chatting with humans, and controlling a robotic arm. With a single neural network, it could switch between these activities using the same underlying weights.

While Gato didn't surpass dedicated systems in performance, it demonstrated a principle: a single model can interface with multiple worlds. It raised the question—could general intelligence emerge not from specialization, but unification?

Case Study: GPT-4 and Agentic Behavior

OpenAI's **GPT-4** showcases startling breadth: writing poetry, solving math problems, passing professional exams, and debugging code. But what's more intriguing is how it's being used in **agentic frameworks** like **AutoGPT** and **BabyAGI**, where language models plan, reason, and execute tasks semi-independently.

These systems combine memory, tool use, and adaptive strategies—early, if brittle, prototypes of AGI-like agents that don't just answer questions but pursue objectives.

Who's Chasing AGI?

Several leading labs openly pursue AGI:

- **OpenAI** aims to build AGI that benefits humanity. Its rapid progress through the GPT series has brought the goal closer to mainstream conversation.
- **DeepMind**, under Google, integrates neuroscience, reinforcement learning, and symbolic reasoning.
- **Anthropic** focuses on safety and alignment, developing scalable, steerable models.
- **Google DeepMind's Gemini** project seeks to unify vision, language, and action into one multimodal system.

These efforts reflect a shared belief: that building broadly capable AI is both a technical and ethical mission.

84

Technical Mountains Yet to Climb

Despite progress, AGI is not around the corner. Key challenges remain:

- **Reasoning**: Most models rely on pattern recognition, not true abstraction
- **Memory**: Long-term planning and contextual awareness are limited
- **Grounding**: AI lacks real-world intuition—its words float above experience
- **Embodiment**: Some argue real intelligence requires a body to interact with the world

---

Case Study: SayCan and PaLM-E Google's **SayCan** links language understanding to robotic actions. Given a goal like "bring me a soda," it evaluates which actions are physically possible and makes a plan. **PaLM-E** goes further, integrating sensory input and proprioception into a single model. These early systems explore what it means to ground intelligence in the real world.

The Alignment Dilemma

With AGI comes the **alignment problem**: how do we ensure machines pursue goals aligned with human values?

Anthropic's Constitutional AI and OpenAI's reinforcement learning from human feedback (RLHF) are attempts to steer models toward safe behavior. Yet these systems can still misinterpret intent, hallucinate facts, or amplify bias.

Case Study: Claude and Constitutional AI Anthropic's **Claude** uses a written set of ethical principles to govern its responses. Instead of learning purely from human ratings, it judges its own behavior against a "constitution." This approach opens new avenues in self-guided alignment—but also new questions about whose values get encoded.

Fear, Hype, and Pause

In 2023, a group of AI leaders—including Elon Musk and Yoshua Bengio—signed an open letter calling for a pause on models more powerful than GPT-4. The letter warned of "profound risks to society and humanity" and urged for safety standards, transparency, and oversight.

Some saw the letter as prudent. Others saw it as posturing. But it underscored one truth: AGI is no longer just a research goal—it's a global concern.

Are We Close?

Predictions vary wildly:

- **Optimists**: AGI by the 2030s
- **Skeptics**: Centuries—or never

Case Study: AGI Benchmarks To evaluate progress, researchers are developing tests like **BIG-bench, AGIEval**, and the **ARC Challenge**—assessing creativity, reasoning, and adaptability. These tests move beyond accuracy to measure cognitive flexibility. So far, no model has cleared the bar for true generality.

The road ahead may involve scaling, new architectures, or entirely different approaches—perhaps even integrating symbolic logic, neuroscience, or evolutionary principles.

A Mirror and a Warning

Whether AGI is near or far, its pursuit reshapes how we define intelligence, autonomy, and consciousness. It forces us to ask: what do we value in being human? What should we build, and why?

AGI is a mirror. It reflects our hopes for mastery, fears of loss, and dreams of transcendence. It is also a warning—that power without purpose, or understanding without alignment, could lead to outcomes we never intended.

In the final chapter, we'll explore a more optimistic vision: not rivalry with intelligent machines, but **coexistence**—a future where humans and AI learn to build, create, and thrive together.

Chapter 12

Coexistence

The Human-AI Partnership: A New Kind of Collaboration

Artificial intelligence is no longer confined to laboratories or servers—it is becoming our co-pilot in daily life. As machines grow more capable, the question isn't whether they'll replace us, but how we'll work alongside them. The most compelling vision of the future isn't humans versus machines—it's humans **with** machines.

In this final chapter, we explore what it means to live and work with AI, not as tools or threats, but as partners. From medicine and education to creativity and care, we'll examine how intelligent systems are already enhancing human potential—and how we can design that future with purpose, empathy, and wisdom.

AI as Ally in Work and Discovery

Rather than displacing people, AI is increasingly playing a supportive role—enhancing human expertise, improving accuracy, and unlocking discoveries that would be impossible alone.

Case Study: Google Health and Radiology In a landmark study published in *Nature*, Google's AI outperformed radiologists in detecting breast cancer from mammograms. But the greatest success came from **human-AI collaboration**: when radiologists and AI worked together, detection accuracy rose even higher. The future of diagnostics is not machine or human—it's both.

Case Study: IBM Watson in Drug Discovery Researchers use IBM Watson to comb through mountains of biomedical data, uncovering hidden relationships between genes, diseases, and compounds. Far from replacing scientists, Watson acts as an accelerator—suggesting hypotheses, not conclusions.

Creative Symbiosis

AI is becoming a collaborator in art, music, writing, and design—amplifying human imagination without replacing it.

Case Study: Ryan Reynolds and ChatGPT For a Mint Mobile commercial, actor Ryan Reynolds asked ChatGPT to write the script in his voice. The result—funny, self-aware, and on-brand—required only light editing. It was a moment of creative fusion: a human voice, echoed through a machine.

Case Study: Coca-Cola's Create Real Magic Campaign Coca-Cola launched an AI art platform using DALL·E and GPT-4, allowing users to remix its iconic visuals into custom artwork. It turned branding into co-creation, making fans part of the creative process.

These examples show that AI doesn't diminish originality—it broadens the stage for participation.

Building Trustworthy Partnerships

For AI to be a reliable partner, it must be designed for **trust**. That includes:

- **Transparency**: Clear reasoning behind decisions
- **Fairness**: Equitable treatment across users and groups
- **Oversight**: Humans accountable for outcomes

Case Study: HireVue's AI in Hiring HireVue used AI to assess job candidates via video interviews. Following public scrutiny over potential bias, it removed facial analysis and introduced ethical audits. The message: trust grows from transparency, not opacity.

Learning Together

AI is transforming education, not by replacing teachers, but by personalizing instruction and expanding access.

Case Study: Khanmigo and Adaptive Tutoring Khan Academy's AI tutor, Khanmigo, guides students through problems with Socratic questions. It adjusts to each learner's pace, nudging them toward deeper understanding.

For teachers, it's a co-instructor. For students, a tireless study partner.

Case Study: AlphaFold's Global Impact DeepMind's AlphaFold predicted the structure of nearly every known protein—releasing the data freely. Researchers worldwide now use it to design medicines, study diseases, and explore biology in ways previously unimaginable. AI became not just a tool, but a global collaborator.

Empathy and Emotional Support

AI is beginning to understand the human emotional landscape. While it can't feel, it can be trained to respond with sensitivity.

Case Study: Woebot and Mental Health Woebot offers cognitive behavioral therapy in chatbot form—guiding users through journaling, self-reflection, and thought reframing. Studies show it can reduce anxiety and depression symptoms, especially for those without access to traditional care.

Case Study: Replika as Companion Replika users engage with AI friends who listen, validate, and converse. Some find comfort. Others seek reflection. It's not a replacement for real relationships—but in moments of loneliness, it can be a lifeline.

The Enduring Human Role

As AI expands its reach, what remains uniquely ours?

- **Curiosity**: The drive to explore the unknown
- **Ethics**: The compass that guides our choices
- **Empathy**: The heart behind our actions
- **Purpose**: The meaning we assign to life

Case Study: Human Moderators in AI Systems Despite advances in content moderation AI, platforms still rely on human reviewers. Machines struggle with nuance—sarcasm, cultural context, moral gray areas. Human judgment remains essential.

We don't compete with AI on speed or scale—we complement it with perspective, care, and conscience.

Designing a Shared Future

To coexist with AI, we must do more than innovate—we must **educate, regulate, and collaborate**.

Case Study: Finland's National AI Curriculum Finland launched "Elements of AI," a free online course to teach citizens the basics of artificial intelligence. Over a million people have taken it, from students to seniors. The course has been translated into 20+ languages. It's a model of inclusive digital literacy.

Global Cooperation From the EU's AI Act to UNESCO's ethical guidelines, governments are beginning to shape AI policy. The challenge ahead is balancing innovation with accountability, freedom with fairness.

From Users to Partners

We once built machines to obey. Now we're building machines that advise, interpret, and adapt. As this shift accelerates, we face a choice: do we design for dependence— or for partnership?

The most transformative AI will not replace us. It will work with us—challenging our assumptions, supporting our ambitions, and extending what it means to be human.

We are not just writing the future of technology—we are co-authoring the future of intelligence.

Epilogue

Intelligence, Imagined Together

We began this journey with a dream—the age-old human fascination with creating intelligence outside ourselves. From mechanical automata to digital neural networks, from logic puzzles to self-learning systems, we've sought to understand and replicate the thing that defines us most: the capacity to think, to learn, to create.

But as we've seen, artificial intelligence is not just a technological phenomenon. It is a philosophical mirror. A societal accelerant. A canvas for our ambitions and our anxieties. And it is a reminder that every tool we create is, in some way, a reflection of who we are—and who we hope to become.

Throughout this book, we've traced the arc of AI from its origins in logic and theory, through its modern incarnations in algorithms and neural networks, to its ever-evolving role in science, creativity, ethics, and everyday life. We've seen how machines now write, paint, move, decide, and assist—not in isolation, but increasingly in collaboration with us.

The question that now remains is not whether AI will shape our future. It already is. The real question is: **how?**

Will we build AI that deepens understanding or spreads misinformation? That empowers the many or serves the few? That aligns with human values—or drifts away from them?

The answers lie not just in the hands of engineers and technologists, but in educators, policymakers, designers, artists, and citizens. In all of us.

AGI may remain on the horizon, but intelligence—artificial or otherwise—is no longer something we can afford to imagine apart from our human story. It's time to imagine it **together.**

So let us:

- Build with responsibility, not just speed
- Design for humanity, not just performance
- Educate not only about how AI works—but why it matters
- Invite everyone to the table, because the future belongs to all of us

AI may extend our cognition. But it is our compassion, our creativity, and our conscience that must guide it.

In the end, the most powerful intelligence we can create will not be the one that thinks the fastest or calculates the most—but the one that helps us become more thoughtful, more just, and more connected than ever before.

Gratitude and Goodbye

If you're reading this final page, thank you, truly.

Writing this book has been as much a process of discovery as it has been of explanation. It's been a conversation, between disciplines, between ideas, and most importantly, between us. Though we may never meet, this shared space of curiosity and reflection has been deeply meaningful to me.

Artificial intelligence is a complex, evolving force. It raises as many questions as it answers. My hope was to make those questions feel accessible, engaging, and worth pondering— not just as a technical subject, but as a human one.

Whether you came here out of wonder, worry, ambition, or awe, I'm grateful you joined me. I hope this book gave you not just clarity, but perspective. Not just understanding, but a sense of agency. Because the future of intelligence, artificial or otherwise, isn't something we wait for. It's something we build.

As we move forward into an age shaped by code, cognition, and creativity, may we do so with intention. Let's be brave enough to innovate, humble enough to listen, and wise enough to ask the right questions.

Thank you for your time, your attention, and your mind. With gratitude,

Edwin Crowe

Appendices A to I

Deeper Dive Reference Guide

Appendix A

Key Concepts in AI

This appendix offers a clear, technically grounded reference to foundational concepts in artificial intelligence. These definitions are structured to support deeper understanding for readers seeking to navigate AI's terminology and principles with confidence.

Artificial Intelligence (AI)

A broad discipline concerned with creating machines capable of performing tasks that typically require human intelligence. These tasks include reasoning, perception, decision-making, problem-solving, and language understanding. AI encompasses subfields such as machine learning, robotics, and natural language processing.

Machine Learning (ML)

A subset of AI focused on developing algorithms that allow computers to learn from data. Machine learning enables systems to make predictions or decisions based on experience, rather than relying solely on fixed, rule-based programming.

Deep Learning (DL)

A subfield of machine learning that leverages artificial neural networks with many layers (hence "deep") to model high-level abstractions in data. Deep learning powers most state-of-the-art AI systems today, particularly in image recognition, speech processing, and natural language tasks.

Model vs. Algorithm

- **Model**: A mathematical representation trained on data to perform a task (e.g., a neural network that classifies images).
- **Algorithm**: The procedure or method used to train the model (e.g., stochastic gradient descent). The algorithm adjusts the model's parameters based on data.

Supervised Learning

A learning paradigm in which a model is trained on input-output pairs (labeled data). The model learns to map inputs (e.g., images) to known outputs (e.g., labels like "cat" or "dog"). Used for classification and regression tasks.

Unsupervised Learning

Here, the model is trained on input data without explicit labels. It must find patterns or structures on its own—such as clustering similar data points or reducing dimensionality. Common methods include k-means clustering and principal component analysis.

101

Reinforcement Learning (RL)

A feedback-driven learning approach in which an agent interacts with an environment, receives rewards or penalties, and learns to optimize its actions over time. It's widely used in robotics, gaming (e.g., AlphaGo), and autonomous systems.

Parameters and Weights

Internal numerical values of a model that are adjusted during training to minimize error. In neural networks, **weights** determine the strength of connections between neurons across layers. **Parameters** is a broader term that includes weights and other adjustable values.

Overfitting and Underfitting

- **Overfitting**: The model performs well on training data but poorly on unseen data. It has memorized patterns too closely.
- **Underfitting**: The model fails to capture meaningful patterns in the training data, resulting in poor performance overall.

Generalization

The model's ability to perform well on data it has never seen before. A well-generalized model avoids both overfitting and underfitting and makes reliable predictions in the real world.

Embeddings

Low-dimensional, continuous vector representations of data—particularly useful in NLP and vision. For instance, word embeddings place semantically similar words closer together in vector space (e.g., "king" and "queen").

Tokens

The smallest units of text processed by language models. A token might be a character, a word, or a subword depending on the tokenizer. For example, "artificial" might be split into "arti" and "ficial" in some systems.

Bias and Variance

- **Bias**: Error introduced by simplifying assumptions in the model. High bias can lead to underfitting.
- **Variance**: Error from excessive sensitivity to small variations in the training data. High variance can lead to overfitting.
- The **bias-variance tradeoff** is a fundamental tension in model design.

Inference vs. Training

- **Training**: The process of optimizing a model using data to learn parameters.
- **Inference**: The deployment phase, where the trained model is used to make predictions on new, unseen inputs.

Appendix B

Neural Network Architectures

Neural networks are the computational heart of modern artificial intelligence. Inspired by the interconnected neurons in biological brains, these architectures allow machines to recognize patterns, represent complex relationships, and learn from data in increasingly human-like ways.

This appendix presents a refined overview of the most influential neural network architectures, explaining how they work, where they're used, and why they matter.

1. Perceptron and Feedforward Neural Networks (FNNs)

- **Perceptron**: The foundational building block of neural networks. A simple unit that computes a weighted sum of inputs and passes it through an activation function (e.g., step or sigmoid). Capable of solving linearly separable problems.
- **Feedforward Neural Networks (Multilayer Perceptrons)**: Extend perceptrons by adding multiple layers. Information flows in one direction—from input to output—without loops. These networks are used for basic classification, regression, and function approximation tasks.

Key Features: Layered structure, non-linear activations (ReLU, tanh), backpropagation for training.

---

2. Convolutional Neural Networks (CNNs)

- Designed specifically for image and spatial data, CNNs learn to detect edges, textures, shapes, and high-level visual features.
- **Convolutional layers** apply small filters (kernels) that slide over the input to extract local patterns.
- **Pooling layers** reduce dimensionality and focus on the most relevant features.

Applications: Image classification, object detection, facial recognition, medical imaging, video analysis.

Key Innovation: Local receptive fields, shared weights, spatial hierarchy.

---

3. Recurrent Neural Networks (RNNs) and Variants

RNNs are designed to process **sequential data**, where previous inputs affect future outputs.

- Maintain a **hidden state** that carries context through time steps.
- Struggle with long-term dependencies due to vanishing gradients.

Advanced Variants:

- **LSTM (Long Short-Term Memory):** Introduces memory cells and gating mechanisms to retain information over longer sequences.
- **GRU (Gated Recurrent Unit):** A simplified LSTM with fewer parameters and similar performance.

Applications: Language modeling, speech recognition, time-series prediction, music generation.

Key Innovation: Sequence awareness through internal memory.

---

4. Transformer Architecture

- Introduced in 2017, transformers revolutionized NLP by replacing recurrence with **self-attention**—a mechanism that allows models to weigh the importance of every word (or token) in a sequence relative to others.
- Enables parallel processing of entire sequences during training, making them far more scalable than RNNs.

Key Components: Multi-head self-attention, positional encoding, feedforward layers, layer normalization.

Applications: Language models (BERT, GPT series, T5), code generation, protein folding (AlphaFold), multimodal reasoning.

Key Innovation: Self-attention for global context and parallelism.

---

5. Encoder-Decoder Frameworks

- A dual-architecture system where the **encoder** compresses input into a context representation, and the **decoder** generates output based on this representation.
- Widely used in sequence-to-sequence tasks.

Applications: Machine translation, image captioning, summarization, chatbots.

Enhancement: The addition of attention layers between encoder and decoder allows models to dynamically focus on relevant input segments while generating each output token.

---

6. Generative Architectures

Autoencoders

- Learn to compress (encode) and reconstruct (decode) input data.
- Useful for anomaly detection, denoising, and dimensionality reduction.

Variational Autoencoders (VAEs)

- Extend autoencoders with probabilistic modeling.
- Learn distributions over latent variables, enabling data generation and interpolation.

Generative Adversarial Networks (GANs)

- Comprise a **generator** (creates data) and a **discriminator** (evaluates realism).
- Trained in a game-like setting until the generator can fool the discriminator.

Applications: Deepfake generation, art synthesis, data augmentation, super-resolution.

Key Innovation: Adversarial training dynamics that produce sharp, realistic outputs.

---

7. Diffusion Models

- A newer class of generative models that learn to reverse a gradual noise-adding process.
- Training involves teaching the model to denoise corrupted inputs step-by-step.

Applications: Image generation (e.g., DALL·E 2, Stable Diffusion), audio synthesis, inpainting.

Key Strength: High-fidelity, diverse sample generation with strong controllability.

Neural Network Architecture Summary Table

Architecture	Best For	Notable Models
Feedforward	Simple classification/regression	Basic MLPs
CNN	Images, spatial data	AlexNet, ResNet, EfficientNet
RNN/LSTM/GRU	Sequences	DeepSpeech, WaveNet
Transformer	Language, code, multimodal	BERT, GPT-4, T5, PaLM
Autoencoder	Representation learning	Denoising AE, VAE
GAN	Realistic generation	StyleGAN, BigGAN
Diffusion	High-quality generation	DALL·E 2, Imagen, Stable Diffusion

These neural architectures form the foundation of today's most advanced AI systems. By understanding their structure, capabilities, and limitations, we gain insight into the strengths and subtleties of modern machine intelligence—and the innovations still to come.

Appendix C

Learning Algorithms and Optimization

Learning algorithms and optimization techniques form the computational core of modern artificial intelligence. These mechanisms govern how models update their internal parameters to minimize error and improve performance. This appendix presents the key ideas that drive learning in neural networks, from gradient descent to regularization and beyond.

---

1. Gradient Descent

Gradient descent is the foundational optimization algorithm used in training nearly all machine learning models. It operates by iteratively adjusting a model's parameters in the direction that minimizes the loss function.

Variants:

- **Stochastic Gradient Descent (SGD)**: Updates weights using a single data point at a time, introducing stochasticity that can help escape local minima.

- **Mini-Batch Gradient Descent**: Processes small batches of data per update, offering a balance between noise and stability.
- **Batch Gradient Descent**: Uses the entire dataset for each update—accurate but computationally intensive.

2. Loss Functions

The loss function quantifies the difference between the model's predictions and the actual targets. It is the quantity that optimization algorithms aim to minimize.

Common Loss Functions:

- **Mean Squared Error (MSE)**: Used for regression; penalizes larger errors more heavily.
- **Cross-Entropy Loss**: Used in classification; measures the dissimilarity between predicted and true probability distributions.
- **Hinge Loss**: Employed in margin-based classifiers like SVMs.
- **Kullback-Leibler (KL) Divergence**: Compares two probability distributions; useful in generative modeling and information theory.

3. Activation Functions

Activation functions introduce non-linearity into neural networks, allowing them to learn complex mappings.

Widely Used Functions:

- **ReLU (Rectified Linear Unit):** $f(x) = \max(0, x)$; fast and efficient, standard in deep networks.
- **Sigmoid:** Compresses input into $(0, 1)$; useful in binary outputs but prone to vanishing gradients.
- **Tanh:** Similar to sigmoid but centered around zero.
- **Softmax:** Converts raw logits into probabilities for multi-class classification.

---

4. Backpropagation

Backpropagation is the algorithm that enables efficient training of deep networks. It applies the **chain rule** of calculus to propagate error gradients backward through the network and compute updates for each parameter.

Combined with gradient descent, backpropagation allows networks to learn from labeled data in supervised learning settings.

---

5. Optimization Algorithms (Optimizers)

Optimizers are methods that update model weights to minimize the loss function, often improving upon plain gradient descent with adaptive strategies.

Common Optimizers:

- **SGD**: Basic and robust, but sensitive to learning rate and slow to converge.
- **Momentum**: Accelerates SGD by dampening oscillations and carrying forward update direction.
- **RMSProp**: Scales learning rates based on the average of recent squared gradients.
- **Adam (Adaptive Moment Estimation)**: Combines momentum and adaptive learning rates; widely used for its stability and efficiency.

---

6. Regularization Techniques

Regularization helps models generalize by discouraging overfitting to training data.

Key Techniques:

- **L2 Regularization (Weight Decay)**: Adds a penalty proportional to the square of the weights.
- **Dropout**: Randomly disables neurons during training to promote redundancy and robustness.
- **Early Stopping**: Halts training when performance on validation data begins to degrade.
- **Batch Normalization**: Normalizes activations within layers to stabilize and speed up training.

7. Learning Rate and Scheduling

The **learning rate** determines how large each weight update is during training. Choosing the right learning rate is crucial to convergence and performance.

Learning Rate Schedulers:

- **Step Decay**: Drops the learning rate at predefined intervals.
- **Exponential Decay**: Reduces the rate gradually over time.
- **Cosine Annealing / Warm Restarts**: Periodically resets or varies the rate to encourage exploration and escape local minima.

Summary: Training Workflow

1. **Initialize** model weights.
2. Perform a **forward pass** to compute predictions.
3. Calculate the **loss** comparing predictions to targets.
4. Apply **backpropagation** to compute gradients.
5. Use an **optimizer** to update parameters.
6. Repeat over many **epochs** across training data.

Optimization and learning algorithms are the engines of artificial intelligence. They translate mathematical insight into practical results, enabling machines to adapt, improve, and perform at scale. Understanding them is key to mastering the art and science of AI.

Appendix D

Data in AI Systems

Data is the bedrock of artificial intelligence. Every prediction, recommendation, and generated response produced by an AI system depends on the data it has seen and how that data has been structured, labeled, and interpreted. In this appendix, we explore the full lifecycle of data in AI systems—from acquisition and preprocessing to the infrastructure that makes large-scale data use possible.

---

1. Data Collection

The quality and representativeness of data profoundly influence the performance and fairness of AI models.

Common Sources:

- Public and private databases
- Web scraping and APIs
- IoT sensors, mobile devices, satellites
- Crowdsourced data
- Simulated environments (e.g., synthetic training data for robotics or autonomous vehicles)

Key Considerations:

- Legal: Licensing, copyright, and data usage rights
- Ethical: Informed consent, privacy, surveillance
- Practical: Cost, scale, refresh frequency

---

2. Data Preprocessing

Before training can begin, raw data must be cleaned, structured, and standardized.

Typical Steps:

- **Data cleaning**: Remove duplicates, handle missing or inconsistent entries
- **Normalization**: Scale features to a common range (e.g., 0–1)
- **Standardization**: Rescale based on mean and standard deviation
- **Encoding**: Convert categorical variables into numeric format (e.g., one-hot, label encoding)
- **Text preprocessing**: Tokenization, lowercasing, stopword removal
- **Image/audio processing**: Resizing, cropping, format conversion

---

3. Feature Engineering

Transforming raw data into meaningful inputs that models can learn from.

Manual Techniques:

- Statistical features (mean, median, standard deviation)
- Ratios and domain-specific combinations
- Polynomial or interaction terms

Automated Approaches:

- Feature selection algorithms (e.g., recursive feature elimination)
- Deep learning-based representation learning

Note: While traditional ML heavily relied on manual feature engineering, modern deep learning learns features directly from raw inputs.

---

4. Dataset Partitioning

Splitting data ensures models are evaluated fairly and avoid overfitting.

- **Training set**: Used to train the model's parameters
- **Validation set**: Used for tuning hyperparameters and detecting overfitting

- **Test set**: Used for final evaluation of performance on truly unseen data

Best Practice: Stratified sampling and cross-validation to preserve class balance.

---

5. Data Labeling and Annotation

Labeling is essential for supervised learning—and often the most time-intensive task.

Methods:

- **Manual annotation**: Human labelers tag data based on guidelines
- **Weak supervision**: Use heuristics, rules, or existing models to generate approximate labels
- **Active learning**: The model selects uncertain examples for human annotation

Tooling:

- Prodigy, Label Studio, Scale AI, Snorkel

---

6. Text and Language Data

Language data requires preprocessing to convert natural text into structured inputs.

Techniques:

- **Tokenization**: Break text into words, subwords, or characters
- **Subword units**: Byte Pair Encoding (BPE), WordPiece—important for handling rare words
- **Embeddings**: Convert tokens into dense vectors using methods like Word2Vec, GloVe, or contextual embeddings from BERT

Modern LLMs rely on vast, multilingual corpora and sophisticated tokenization schemes to understand and generate human-like text.

---

7. Image and Audio Data

Visual and auditory data require modality-specific treatment.

Images:

- Standardize resolution and color channels
- Augment with flips, crops, rotations, noise injection

Audio:

- Convert waveforms to spectrograms, MFCCs
- Normalize loudness, trim silence, resample to fixed rate

---

8. Data Augmentation

Improves generalization by creating slightly altered versions of existing data.

Examples:

- **Vision**: Random crops, brightness shifts, Gaussian noise
- **Text**: Back-translation, synonym replacement, paraphrasing
- **Audio**: Time stretching, pitch shifting, adding background noise

Augmentation is crucial in domains where labeled data is scarce or expensive to obtain.

---

9. Data Quality and Bias

Garbage in, garbage out. The integrity and inclusiveness of training data directly affect model fairness and reliability.

Issues to Watch:

- **Sampling bias**: Certain populations underrepresented
- **Label bias**: Subjectivity, inconsistency, cultural assumptions
- **Temporal bias**: Data becomes stale over time (concept drift)

Best Practices:

- Auditing datasets for demographic balance
- Monitoring data drift and updating as needed
- Annotator training and documentation

---

10. Big Data and Infrastructure

Scaling up requires specialized tools and platforms.

Infrastructure Components:

- **Storage**: Cloud buckets (S3), distributed filesystems (HDFS)
- **Processing**: Apache Spark, Ray, Dask
- **Orchestration**: Airflow, Prefect, Kubeflow
- **Versioning & Tracking**: DVC, MLflow, Weights & Biases

Mature AI organizations invest heavily in data engineering and MLOps to support continuous learning and deployment.

Data is not just the input to AI—it is its foundation, its teacher, and its mirror. Understanding how it's collected, processed, and preserved is essential to building AI that performs accurately, adapts responsibly, and serves all.

Appendix E

Evaluation Metrics

Evaluating the performance of AI systems is as critical as building them. Metrics provide the tools to quantify how well a model performs, how it behaves under different conditions, and how it aligns with practical goals and ethical standards. This appendix surveys the most widely used evaluation metrics across different AI tasks, with guidance on their use and interpretation.

---

1. Classification Metrics

For tasks where inputs are mapped to discrete categories (e.g., spam detection, image classification).

Confusion Matrix

A breakdown of predicted vs. actual outcomes:

- **True Positives (TP)**: Correctly predicted positives
- **True Negatives (TN)**: Correctly predicted negatives
- **False Positives (FP)**: Incorrectly predicted positives (Type I error)
- **False Negatives (FN)**: Missed actual positives (Type II error)

Derived Metrics:

- **Accuracy** = (TP + TN) / Total
- **Precision** = TP / (TP + FP) → Correctness of positive predictions
- **Recall** = TP / (TP + FN) → Coverage of actual positives
- **F1 Score** = 2 × (Precision × Recall) / (Precision + Recall)

Tip: Use F1 when classes are imbalanced or false negatives are costly.

---

2. Regression Metrics

Used when the output is continuous rather than categorical (e.g., predicting housing prices).

- **Mean Absolute Error (MAE)**: Average magnitude of errors without direction
- **Mean Squared Error (MSE)**: Penalizes larger errors more heavily
- **Root Mean Squared Error (RMSE)**: Square root of MSE; more interpretable
- **R² Score (Coefficient of Determination)**: Proportion of variance explained by the model (1 is ideal)

Note: RMSE emphasizes large errors; MAE provides a more robust average.

3. Ranking and Retrieval Metrics

Common in recommendation systems, information retrieval, and search engines.

- **Precision@k**: Fraction of top-k items that are relevant
- **Recall@k**: Fraction of relevant items retrieved in top-k
- **Mean Average Precision (MAP)**: Averages precision across relevant items for ranked lists
- **Normalized Discounted Cumulative Gain (NDCG)**: Captures both rank order and relevance scores

Use Case: Ideal for systems where the position of the result matters.

---

4. Generative and Language Model Metrics

When outputs are generated (text, image, audio), exact answers may not exist—so evaluation is more nuanced.

For Text:

- **Perplexity**: Measures how surprised the model is by the actual text (lower is better)
- **BLEU**: N-gram overlap for translation tasks
- **ROUGE**: Recall-focused n-gram overlap, often used in summarization

- **METEOR**: Considers synonymy, stemming, and alignment
- **BERTScore**: Uses contextual embeddings to capture semantic similarity

For Images:

- **Inception Score (IS)**: Measures both clarity and diversity of generated images
- **Fréchet Inception Distance (FID)**: Compares generated and real image distributions

Caution: These metrics don't capture all aspects of human perception or coherence.

---

5. Calibration and Confidence

Models that output probabilities should be evaluated on whether those probabilities reflect real-world outcomes.

- **Brier Score**: Measures the accuracy of predicted probabilities
- **Expected Calibration Error (ECE)**: Compares confidence to actual accuracy
- **Reliability Diagrams**: Plots prediction confidence vs. observed accuracy

Importance: Crucial for safety-critical applications like medicine or finance.

6. Human Evaluation

When quantitative metrics fall short, human judgment fills the gap—especially for language, creativity, and user experience.

Methods:

- **Likert-scale ratings**: Fluency, relevance, coherence
- **A/B testing**: Preference between system outputs
- **Task success**: How well the system helps achieve a real-world goal

Limitations: Subjective, costly, and less scalable—but often indispensable.

---

7. Fairness and Bias Metrics

Evaluating equity across different subgroups is essential for responsible AI.

- **Demographic Parity**: Outcome independence from sensitive attributes
- **Equalized Odds**: Equal error rates across groups
- **Calibration by Group**: Predictive confidence is equally accurate for all subgroups

Use with Context: Trade-offs often exist between fairness, accuracy, and utility.

Choosing the Right Metrics

The best metric depends on the task, audience, and constraints. Accuracy alone rarely tells the full story. Metrics define what we value and optimize—so they must be chosen with both care and clarity.

Key Principle: Always align your evaluation strategy with real-world objectives and potential harms.

Appendix F

Foundations of Explainability

As AI systems grow more powerful and integrated into daily life, the need to interpret and explain their decisions becomes paramount. Explainable AI (XAI) addresses this need by making machine learning models more transparent, interpretable, and accountable—especially in high-stakes domains like healthcare, finance, law, and autonomous systems.

This appendix introduces the foundational principles, tools, and trade-offs behind explainability in AI.

---

1. Why Explainability Matters

- **Trust and Transparency**: Users and stakeholders are more likely to adopt systems they understand.
- **Debugging and Auditing**: Explanations help diagnose errors, data leakage, or unintended behavior.
- **Regulatory Compliance**: Data protection laws like GDPR require intelligible explanations for automated decisions.
- **Ethical Oversight**: Enhances our ability to detect bias, unfairness, and discrimination.

Without explainability, AI decisions risk becoming opaque, unchallengeable, and potentially unjust.

2. Global vs. Local Explainability

- **Global Explainability**: Describes how the model behaves in general across the dataset. Example: feature importance scores.
- **Local Explainability**: Describes how the model made a particular prediction. Example: why a specific loan application was rejected.

---

3. Model-Agnostic vs. Model-Specific Methods

- **Model-Agnostic Methods**: Work with any type of black-box model by observing input-output behavior (e.g., LIME, SHAP).
- **Model-Specific Methods**: Use internal architecture or gradients (e.g., attention maps in transformers, Grad-CAM in CNNs).

---

4. Popular Techniques

SHAP (SHapley Additive exPlanations)

- Based on Shapley values from cooperative game theory.
- Assigns each feature a contribution value to a specific prediction.
- Offers both local and global interpretations.

LIME (Local Interpretable Model-agnostic Explanations)

- Trains a simple surrogate model around a specific prediction.
- Interprets model behavior in the neighborhood of a data point.

Feature Importance (Global)

- Ranks input features based on their overall contribution to model accuracy.
- Often used in tree-based models like random forests or XGBoost.

Partial Dependence Plots (PDPs)

- Show how the predicted outcome varies with a feature while holding others constant.

Individual Conditional Expectation (ICE) Plots

- Like PDPs but for individual data instances, revealing heterogeneity in effects.

Attention Visualizations

- In transformer models, attention weights can reveal which parts of the input the model is focusing on.

Saliency Maps and Grad-CAM

- Used in CNNs to highlight which regions of an image influenced the model's prediction.
- Helpful in medical imaging, safety-critical visual tasks.

---

5. Tools and Libraries

Tool	Description	Platform
SHAP	Unified framework for feature attribution	Python
LIME	Local surrogate model explanations	Python
Captum	Interpretability for PyTorch models	PyTorch
InterpretML	Microsoft's suite for model interpretability	Python
ELI5	Lightweight explanation tools for classifiers	Python/sklearn

6. Challenges and Trade-offs

- **Approximation Risk**: Post-hoc explanations may not faithfully reflect internal decision-making.
- **Complexity vs. Interpretability**: More powerful models are often harder to explain.
- **Comprehensibility**: Not all explanations are meaningful to non-experts.
- **Computational Cost**: Some explanation methods are expensive, especially for deep models.

Effective explainability balances technical fidelity with human understanding.

Explainability is more than a tool—it is a commitment to transparency, fairness, and accountability in the age of intelligent systems. As AI influences more of our lives, ensuring that decisions can be understood and questioned is essential to building responsible and human-centered technology.

Appendix H

Prominent Benchmarks and Datasets

Understanding and evaluating artificial intelligence requires access to robust, standardized datasets and benchmarks. These resources drive progress by providing consistent challenges across fields and enabling fair comparison between models. This appendix offers a categorized overview of the most influential datasets and evaluation suites in AI.

1. Vision Benchmarks

MNIST

- Handwritten digits dataset (0–9), grayscale, 28x28 pixels.
- Widely used for image classification basics and model prototyping.

CIFAR-10 / CIFAR-100

- Small images (32x32) of real-world objects in 10 or 100 categories.
- Useful for image classification and early vision tasks.

ImageNet

- Large-scale dataset (14M+ images, 21K+ categories).
- Drove the deep learning revolution in vision via the ImageNet Large Scale Visual Recognition Challenge (ILSVRC).
- Models: AlexNet, ResNet, EfficientNet, Vision Transformers (ViT).

COCO (Common Objects in Context)

- Object detection, segmentation, and captioning.
- Includes bounding boxes and natural image contexts.
- Used extensively in object recognition competitions.

Open Images

- Google's dataset with millions of annotated images.
- Supports object detection, segmentation, visual relationships.

---

2. Language Benchmarks

GLUE (General Language Understanding Evaluation)

- Measures model performance across tasks like sentiment analysis, paraphrasing, inference, and more.
- Popularized transformer benchmarking.

SuperGLUE

- More challenging successor to GLUE, featuring nuanced language tasks.
- Designed to test "human-like" understanding.

SQuAD (Stanford Question Answering Dataset)

- Focused on reading comprehension and extractive question answering.
- SQuAD 2.0 includes unanswerable questions for robustness.

CNN/DailyMail

- Summarization dataset built from news articles and bullet-point summaries.

The Pile

- Large, diverse text dataset (825GB) used to pretrain large language models.
- Includes academic papers, web data, books, GitHub, etc.

3. Multimodal Benchmarks

VQA (Visual Question Answering)

- Combines vision and language: models must answer questions about images.
- Encourages grounding and cross-modal reasoning.

LAION-5B

- Massive image–text dataset used to train CLIP and Stable Diffusion.
- Open, web-scale, enabling foundational model research in vision-language.

COCO Captions / Flickr30K

- Datasets pairing images with human-written descriptions.
- Useful for training and evaluating image captioning models.

---

4. Speech and Audio Datasets

LibriSpeech

- Derived from public-domain audiobooks.
- Widely used in automatic speech recognition (ASR).

Common Voice (Mozilla)

- Multilingual, crowdsourced speech dataset.
- Designed to diversify speech data across accents and languages.

---

5. Specialized Domains

AlphaFold Protein Structure Database

- Predictions for hundreds of thousands of proteins using AlphaFold.
- Accelerates research in biology, medicine, and chemistry.

MIMIC-III / MIMIC-IV

- De-identified electronic health records (EHR) for ICU patients.
- Used in AI-driven healthcare research.

ARC (AI2 Reasoning Challenge)

- Grade-school science questions requiring reasoning and world knowledge.
- Tests logic, inference, and symbolic reasoning in AI.

---

6. Meta-Evaluation and Leaderboards

HELM (Holistic Evaluation of Language Models)

- Stanford-led framework for testing LLMs across accuracy, bias, robustness, efficiency, and more.

BIG-bench (Beyond the Imitation Game)

- A collaborative benchmark evaluating LLMs across 200+ diverse tasks.
- Explores abstraction, reasoning, multilinguality, humor, and ethics.

Papers with Code

- Hosts benchmark leaderboards and links to open-source models and datasets.
- A valuable real-time tool for tracking state-of-the-art performance.

Notes for Readers

- These datasets and benchmarks evolve rapidly—many are expanded, retired, or supplemented each year.
- Always check licensing and usage terms before working with real data, especially in medical, legal, or sensitive domains.
- Benchmark saturation (e.g., models nearing 100% on some tasks) has led researchers to develop more nuanced and diverse evaluation tools, pushing beyond accuracy alone.

Appendix I

The Timeline of AI

1940s–1950s: The Foundations

- 1943 – McCulloch & Pitts propose the first mathematical model of an artificial neuron.
- 1950 – Alan Turing publishes "Computing Machinery and Intelligence", proposing the Turing Test.
- 1956 – Dartmouth Conference marks the birth of AI as a field, coined by John McCarthy.

1960s–1970s: Early Hype and Limitations

- 1966 – ELIZA, a rule-based "therapist" chatbot, shows early NLP capabilities.
- 1970s – Expert systems (e.g., MYCIN) dominate AI research with hand-coded rules.
- Late 1970s – First AI Winter begins as progress stalls and funding dries up.

1980s: Knowledge Engineering and Neural Network Revival

- 1980s – Boom in expert systems, especially in industry.
- 1986 – Backpropagation is popularized by Rumelhart, Hinton, and Williams, reviving neural networks.
- 1987–1993 – Second AI Winter triggered by overhype and poor generalization in expert systems.

1990s: Probabilistic AI and Narrow Successes

- 1997 – IBM's Deep Blue defeats chess world champion Garry Kasparov.
- Rise of Bayesian networks and statistical learning methods.
- Early speech recognition and recommender systems enter practical use.

2000s: Data-Driven AI and Web-Scale Learning

- 2006 – Geoffrey Hinton introduces "deep learning" as a term.
- Big data, faster GPUs, and open-source frameworks begin to shape modern AI.
- AI appears in search engines, ads, recommendation engines.

2010s: The Deep Learning Revolution

- 2012 – AlexNet wins ImageNet competition, demonstrating the power of CNNs.
- 2014 – GANs (Generative Adversarial Networks) introduced by Ian Goodfellow.
- 2015 – ResNet deepens CNNs; TensorFlow launches.
- 2016 – AlphaGo defeats human champion Lee Sedol in Go, demonstrating deep reinforcement learning.
- 2017 – "Attention is All You Need" introduces the Transformer architecture.
- 2018 – BERT revolutionizes NLP with bidirectional language understanding.

2020s: Foundation Models and Generative AI

- 2020 – GPT-3 released with 175B parameters; large language models enter public consciousness.
- 2021 – DALL·E, CLIP, Codex show multimodal and coding capabilities.
- 2022 – Stable Diffusion, Midjourney, and ChatGPT bring generative AI to mass users.
- 2023 – GPT-4, Claude, Gemini, LLaMA show multi-expert and multimodal capabilities.
- 2023 – AlphaFold predicts millions of protein structures, transforming biology.
- Growing focus on alignment, safety, and governance for increasingly general models.

Today and Tomorrow

- Research expands toward Artificial General Intelligence (AGI), autonomous agents, multimodal systems, and embodied AI.
  - Questions shift from "Can machines think?" to "How should they think—and work with us?"

---

www.ingramcontent.com/pod-product-compliance
Lightning Source LLC
LaVergne TN
LVHW051652050326
832903LV00032B/3762